From Redundancy to Success

POWERFUL WAYS OF FORGING A NEW CAREER FOLLOWING
REDUNDANCY

About the Author

Tom McGuinness is Chief Executive of the Irish Productivity Centre. He has a Master's Degree in Organisational Behaviour from the Irish Management Institute/Trinity College Dublin. He has worked for over 25 years as an expert consultant designing and implementing change programmes, helping organisations and their employees through the redundancy process. He has extensive experience of the effects of redundancy on people and organisations. He has also written extensively and addressed numerous conferences on organisational change and redundancy.

From Redundancy to Success

POWERFUL WAYS OF FORGING A NEW CAREER
FOLLOWING REDUNDANCY

Tom McGuinness

BLACKHALL
Publishing

This book was typeset by Gough Typesetting for
Blackhall Publishing
27 Carysfort Avenue
Blackrock
Co. Dublin
Ireland
e-mail: info@blackhallpublishing.com
www.blackhallpublishing.com

ISBN: 1 842180 82 7

A catalogue record for this book is available from the British
Library.

Printed in Ireland by
ColourBooks Ltd

Foreword

The continuing boom in the Irish economy sometimes masks the other less appealing aspect – redundancy, despite our significant achievement in creating almost 600,000 new jobs. Over the last decade, many well-known industries both in the private and public sectors have either closed or departed our shores to new locations. In the same period, there have been 185,000 notified redundancies.

Many workers have also experienced the dreaded market demands of rationalisation, downsizing and cost-cutting measures which inevitably entail voluntary or compulsory redundancy.

The most recent social partnership agreement – "Sustaining Progress" – has made substantial changes to the Redundancy Payments Act and previous thresholds. These in turn have granted to employees reasonable redundancy payments to reflect their working contribution to enterprises and services.

Tom McGuinness provides therefore a very timely and visionary guide towards how to use the redundancy situation to the best advantage. By reviewing the wider personal, emotional and psychological aspects of losing or departing one's employment, he gives a wider perspective to this traumatic experience than just the usual financial or legal aspects. He brings an element of vital humanity to the experience.

The tone of this guide to redundancy and its aftermath is positive, encouraging and practical. It is also an invaluable compendium of useful sources of information and an outline of both legal and fiscal entitlements, which is enriched by practical case examples on the major stages of the redundancy process. He describes and provides helpful advice on the supports necessary to re-enter the labour market and the necessity to enhance one's educational opportunities and qualifications.

In *From Redundancy to Success*, Tom McGuinness has produced both an informative and very sympathetic understanding of an aspect of our "Celtic Tiger" that sometimes we fail to understand and appreciate but that will continue to be with us despite our achievements and successes. After all, it is our people who provide us with our competitive advantage in the world economy and they are deserving of our support and understanding in periods of unemployment.

Kieran Mulvey
Chief Executive
Labour Relations Commission

Preface

Redundancy can happen to anyone and it is now part of working life for many people. If it is happening to you, it is important at the outset to realise that you are but one of the many thousands that face this challenge each year. For each individual the prospect is different and will provoke different reactions and responses. This is natural. Whether you have been hearing rumours for months or have been shocked by the unexpected announcement, being made redundant will have had an impact on you.

For some people, facing up to the trauma and emotional upset is the most difficult part; others find the practical realities that result from the loss of income and relative security more problematic. Being made redundant and seeking out new possibilities can be stressful but it is also an opportunity to make change and take control of your own destiny. Change will be an inevitable part of the process. Redundancy provides an opportunity to reappraise your work life and to consider what you want to do in the future. Perhaps you were unhappy anyway, you may have unfulfilled ambitions or you may feel you have not fully realised your potential. This is a chance to do something about it, change certain aspects of your life and realise your goals. Taking time out to reappraise your strengths, to discover what you really want and to make positive plans for the future will be both challenging and exciting.

There are fortunately many examples of people who have moved on to more satisfying and rewarding jobs and careers: some have taken the opportunity to become their own boss; by getting additional educational qualifications, some have created new and exciting job possibilities that they had not been able to avail of before.

To deal effectively with redundancy, as with most other challenges in life, it is important to remain positive, inform yourself as fully as possible, assess your options, generate support and move on in a clearly defined way. Creating the right conditions to turn redundancy into success requires accurate information and taking the right approach at each stage. Harnessing the vast array of support and information services available to you and analysing your situation carefully is vital. Knowing what to do at each stage and how to handle the various challenges that you will meet along the way will give you that advantage so important to achieve success.

The objective of this book is to pull together the various elements of success into a logical sequence of actions to ensure you resume a satisfying and rewarding career. This book will provide practical information, real case examples and powerful strategies that will enable you not only to survive the experience of redundancy but also to triumph through it and make it your gateway to future success.

Contents

Acknowledgements

I would like to acknowledge the many people who provided help and guidance to me in completing this book, most particularly those who recounted their own personal experience of being made redundant but wish for personal reasons to remain anonymous.

My family – wife Frances, children John, Claire and Patrick – were of tremendous support, especially Patrick, who assisted in researching and drafting various sections.

Breeda Finnerty, my colleague in IPC, who took the raw document and made it into a coherent manuscript. Majella Kelleher for her input on stress management.

To those who read the manuscript – Dermot Killen, Smurfit Ireland, Mark Tracey, Ian MacGowan Smyth, Gerry Flannery, Martin Naughton, SIPTU, Shirley Kiernan, EDL Resources plc – and provided valuable feedback, I am most grateful.

While the views expressed in this book are very much my own, IPC, where I have worked for over twenty years, has provided me with a wealth and variety of business and human resource management experience on which this book is based. I would like to acknowledge my colleagues and IPC Council for their support.

Finally, I would like to thank Blackhall Publishing for publishing the outcome of what for me was an exciting and challenging task.

CHAPTER 1

Introduction

Being made redundant has a different effect on everyone. For a fortunate few, it is welcomed as a means of collecting a pot of money and moving on to pastures new. For most, however, it is a traumatic, unsettling experience and, as with all experiences of this nature, people are generally bewildered as to why it is happening to them.

Why do redundancies occur?

Industries come and go and new ones emerge to take their place. Like people, organisations have a natural span of life – what is known as a lifecycle. Unless they renew themselves and provide new products or services that their customers want, they go out of business. New technologies replacing old ones also play a part. Computers and automation have revolutionised both the office and the factory. Emerging countries in Eastern Europe, India and China are now supplying goods and services at lower prices and of good quality. Just think of how many brand names were prominent in the marketplace thirty years ago and that are no longer available. Look at how many companies have disappeared from Ireland in recent years – high profile names such as Digital, Packard Electric, Motorola and Gateway, to name but a few.

In 2003, over 27,000 people faced the prospect of having no job, many in very difficult circumstances. This is a considerable increase over previous years, when redundancy levels were running at around 12,000 every year. Some economists are warning that these higher levels are set to continue for the foreseeable future. One thing is certain: as the economy changes, moving as it is to a high-wage, high-productivity economy, redundancies will continue to be part of the Irish scene for some time to come.

Originally, the Irish economy was based on agriculture. With the decline of agriculture, manufacturing employment took some of the slack. Manufacturing employment will likely decline and growth in service-based jobs will be the way of the future. Service-based jobs require different skills and different mindsets. The very nature of work and the concept of the job will change. Growth will also take place in atypical jobs, many of a part-time nature.

The previous transition from agriculture to industrial-based employment was made successfully and therefore there is every reason to be optimistic about future transitions. However, whether redundancies are happening because of increasing competition from overseas, downturns in the economy or the introduction of new technology is of little comfort to those who have to endure the experience of seeing their job, to which they have devoted so much energy, vanish. This is particularly so as a job is often used to describe the person: he is a fitter; she is banker. Sometimes, a person's occupation is better known than their name.

Change is seldom, if ever, easy. This applies at all stages of life. Yes, in theory, it is easier perhaps for the younger person, but older people have the advantage of experience and, in many cases, can build upon a much wider range of skills. The golden rule is to adopt an optimistic outlook when dealing with the issue of redundancy. This can be easier said than done but, as this book will demonstrate, being made redundant need not be the end of the world but the beginning of a new phase in your life.

Many books and articles have been written from a managerial perspective on how to implement a redundancy programme. These publications are often concerned with the legalities involved and, while these are important, there is more to redundancy than legal issues. Little has been written from the perspective of the individual being made redundant and how they can deal with this event in a positive and constructive way. This is the prime focus of this book.

Understanding redundancy

In today's volatile employment market, the concept of a 'job for life' has all but disappeared. It is forecast that 80 per cent of the technology we use today will be replaced in ten years' time. One remarkable statistic published by the IDA illustrates this well. In 1992, there were 78,000 people employed in the multinational sector in Ireland. Over the subsequent ten years, job losses in this sector amounted to 85,000. Yet, despite this, there are currently 133,000 people employed by multinational companies. This means that nearly 140,000 jobs were created, replacing not just the jobs that were lost but actually increasing the numbers employed.

The level of change is therefore enormous and has tremendous consequences for people in employment. Mergers and acquisitions of long-established companies frequently involve restructuring, with old jobs disappearing and new jobs emerging. Even in the public sector, where jobs are expected to be more stable, outsourcing of services has had an impact on many job categories. No sector is immune from change. As a result, increasing numbers of people are discovering that their careers and jobs are subject to abrupt and seismic change, especially where redundancy is a real possibility.

Redundancy, whether expected or not, has many practical and emotional consequences. Dealing with redundancy is an emotional experience – both for those who lose their jobs and for managers laden with the burden of implementing a redundancy programme. It is highly desirable from the point of view of the employee as well as the public image of the company that redundancies are handled sensitively and in ways that allow those most affected to retain their respect and self-confidence. This is particularly important where redun- dancies are of an arbitrary or involuntary nature and little or no choice is given. Too often, this is handled insensitively. While progressive companies support those being made redundant with advice and assistance, other employers inform their employees summarily or, even worse, employees hear about it first in the media. Many managers are reluctant to deal with redundancy clearly and positively. They retreat into jargon or euphemistic phrases. They end up not stating the clear facts and leaving those affected confused.

This is not only completely unsatisfactory but also distressing, because the impression given is that some anonymous person has callously consigned you and your contribution to the refuse heap. Most importantly, redundancy is never the fault of the individual but rather a reflection of the management of the company or indeed caused by an event outside everyone's control, such as a natural disaster. However, the individual being made redundant may not appreciate this clearly and, as a result, may feel a sense of guilt or, worse still, a sense of worthlessness. A feeling of betrayal is natural in these circumstances. If the redundancy process is mishandled, then this further exacerbates the situation. Redundancy is difficult enough to comprehend without it being handled clumsily.

What is meant by the term redundancy?

Redundancy has a particular meaning and it is important to understand what it is and when it can occur. The following circumstances must prevail:

- The employer has ceased or intends to cease carrying on the business in which the employee was employed, or ceases or intends to cease carrying out this business at the place where the employee was employed.

- The requirements for employees to carry out work of the particular kind in which the person concerned was employed have ceased or diminished or are expected to cease or diminish, either in the business as a whole or where the person was employed.

All of the words used above require explanation and have been defined in law or through case law. Even the word 'dismissal' and the difference between dismissal and resignation are grey areas and have been tested in the courts on many occasions. Further elaboration on the legal aspects is included in the next chapter.

Without going into the finer points of the many circumstances and the differing legal interpretations, the fundamentals for redundancy to be lawful are:

- The reason for dismissal is genuine redundancy.

- The execution of the redundancy is fair and reasonable.

- The selection criteria and the selection process are acceptable and fair.

One thing to bear in mind is that the job or part of the job has disappeared or is about to disappear. As already mentioned, it does not mean that the individual is worthless. Although this will not dull the impact in practical terms, it is an important point to help you to achieve greater peace of mind. The job is not the person but only one aspect of a person. Beginning to see the redundancy situation from this perspective is a vital step in learning to deal with events as they unfold.

Why is the redundancy occurring?

General reasons that redundancy occurs were covered earlier but each situation is different. To come to terms with your redundancy, it is important that you establish just what are the reasons in your particular situation.

- Is it because of changes in the business environment?
- Is it because of policy changes decided locally or at headquarters?
- Is reducing costs the primary concern?
- Is it because of technology?
- Is the product or service being discontinued?

Understanding the 'why' and 'what' will enable you to decide on your next course of action.

- Is the redundancy inevitable?
- Is the redundancy fair?
- Are there alternatives, such as part-time or contract working?
- Should you contest your selection?
- Is it better to accept the reality and move on?

Getting clear information and support is essential as soon as the redundancies are announced. Chapter 2 explains how to do this and deals with the key issues you should address.

Dealing with the Early Stages of Redundancy

Facing up emotionally to redundancy

Very often, your initial reaction to losing your job in this way is similar to that experienced following bereavement. Something central to your life is being abruptly removed, leaving you feeling unsure of yourself, angry, upset and sometimes betrayed. Perhaps you have held the same job or worked for the same company for a considerable number of years and feel totally out of touch with current methods of searching for new job opportunities. Most importantly, the effect of redundancy on your self-esteem leaves you with a feeling of being out of control of your life – someone else is pulling the strings, controlling your destiny, and this makes you feel uncomfortable and even scared of what lies ahead.

You will not be able to move forward until you have faced up to the way you feel about the situation and have taken control again. The support of your family and friends is crucial at this time, so do not attempt to do all the worrying yourself. Those who care about you will want to help, so let them, even if it is just to let them listen while you talk out your concerns and feelings. Listening, empathising and offering support to the individual who has suffered the indignity of redundancy is probably the most important function a family can perform, particularly at the early stages.

Remember, redundancy is not personal, even though it can feel like it is. The causes are invariably outside your control. Feeling sorry for yourself and indeed your colleagues is natural. However, the sooner you turn this negative energy into positive action the better. There are ways to recover and establish yourself on a new and even more exciting career track.

Dealing with the loss

Many who are made redundant testify to it being one of the most distressing experiences of their work life. Why is redundancy so distressing? How can it be so damaging to our self-respect?

While the answer may seem obvious, it is worth exploring why we feel the way we do about this traumatic event. There are many emotions associated with redundancy and they include some of the following:

• Anger

• Guilt

• Self-pity

• Shame

• Chronic indecisiveness

• Lack of self-satisfaction

• Family tension

• Apathy

Feeling these emotions, or a combination thereof, indicates that you may be undergoing a grieving process relating to redundancy. Because redundancy impacts on many important areas of your life, there are good reasons for grieving. Looking at some of these areas will give you a deeper understanding of these feelings.

Personal satisfaction

Having a role within an organisation can be enormously satisfying. To know that your skills and efforts are required and that you play an important part in a wider picture can be immensely rewarding. Redundancy robs us of this feeling.

The social dimension

Work has a strong social dimension to it. It provides an opportunity to be part of a community and, as social animals, we value this very much. Our work colleagues frequently become friends. They are the people with whom we share our aspirations, discuss the issues of the day and share our successes and failures. This sense of community is destroyed by redundancy. It can bring to the surface a sense of vulnerability and leave us insecure. We are in a sense being forced out of our familiar community and into a new community.

Sometimes, a person who has been made redundant feels a certain stigma is attached to them. Associated with redundancy are feelings of rejection that go to the very core of the person's identity. This sense of isolation and rejection can be quite stressful for many. How to deal with resultant stress is outlined in Chapter 11.

Impact on finances

Lack of money can drastically affect the quality of life that the individual and their dependants enjoy. It effects the very environment that we live in from day to day. It is usually very difficult to escape the realities caused by loss of earnings. This can affect our well-being very much for the worse, often imposing difficult pressures on the family and causing a decline in family morale.

Effects on the family

The family may not fully understand or indeed feel the pressures and concerns you are experiencing and may react in a different way than you expect. They may be looking for answers that you do not yet have. They may be anxious to help but may not know how to do this. These and other tensions may, at the outset, make matters worse but working through them in a positive way can yield long-term benefits and improved relationships.

Increasing stress levels

When someone is in the midst of redundancy, morale can be at such a low level that it can seem as if circumstances are conspiring against them. Difficulties seem to multiply. "It never seems to rain but it pours", can represent the mood. Pressures can become extreme. Stress levels rise.

* * *

Change is difficult. When it is beyond our control, it can be a very disorientating experience. Any drastic change can invoke in us turbulent and negative emotions – pain, shame, anger and apathy. Accept that these are natural but do not accept that you will have to live with them for long. It is important that we come to terms with and then overcome these feelings and allow them to be a foundation from which to move forward positively into the future.

The best way to do this is to:

1. Release and confide your feelings to someone you trust

2. Pace yourself: do not rush into the healing process; take time and the transition will be smoother

3. Involve yourself in activities that give a heightened sense of personal satisfaction.

This will help you to gradually rebuild your confidence.

Except for the lucky few who welcome redundancy, being made redundant is almost invariably a shocking experience. Even the so-called lucky few are facing a major transition and will have issues and concerns to address.

The period of notice

When a programme of redundancy is implemented, it is the normal procedure for the employer to give a set period of notice (see Chapter 3). This is often the most difficult time. Morale plummets and it becomes increasingly difficult to keep motivation at even minimum levels. You may become disaffected. The idea that you continue to do your job making a profit for the very organisation that is rejecting you can generate deep emotions of bitterness and anger. You can feel yourself in a kind of limbo – employed to do a job in a business that no longer wants you. Your colleagues may also be depressed and their sense of foreboding may spill over on you.

These feelings are to be expected. Ultimately, working out your notice without unnecessary dramas and recriminations is probably the best way of getting the most out of a bad situation. Maintaining good relationships with your colleagues and particularly those in managerial positions makes good sense, as you may need their support and assistance later on. For example, you will need references from your immediate manager or from the personnel department. They may be able to put you in touch with possible job opportunities. The moral support of your colleagues will be a help to you through this uncertain time. For these and other reasons, unnecessarily damaging relationships built up over a long period could be a mistake in the long term, and avoiding mistakes at this stage is sensible.

Loss of control and feelings of rejection are the hallmarks of the redundancy experience and are frequently accompanied by feelings of anger. Make sure you express the anger you feel in an appropriate way. Use it to energise yourself, to take on the new challenges with gusto and to make positive changes in your life.

Moving on – Goal setting

It is important to redirect your focus as soon as possible from your current uncertain situation to the more positive aspects of the future. Setting a personal goal is an excellent way of focussing your efforts and emotions as you embark on carving out a new and prosperous future for yourself. Initially, this goal should be practical and short term. It could be related to doing up a CV, assessing your financial position or clarifying your entitlements. Everyone will have different goals.

The rules of good goal setting are simple:

• State your goal in clear terms – be specific

• Visualise what is involved and what it will be like when it is achieved

• List the steps to achieve it

• Break down larger goals into smaller ones if possible

• Set out in a systematic way – one step at time

• Make sure your first goal is achievable, as this will build confidence.

You may be driven by a high degree of anxiety at this stage. However, rushing around frantically will not achieve the best result; it is better to take things at a more realistic pace. This will help you avoid making mistakes and setting off in the wrong direction, wasting your valuable time and energy.

As you grow in confidence and your situation becomes clearer, you will be in a better position to consider the bigger picture and set goals for your future career direction. This could be the chance to embark on a new career in an area that, for many reasons, was previously unavailable to you. Perhaps this is an opportunity to explore an area you have always been interested in. Maybe you felt somewhat dissatisfied with your career or job even before you were made redundant. Fear of change may have prevented you from seeking out new opportunities. Being 'pushed off the deep end' makes for a completely new scenario where there are dangers as well as opportunities.

Think about turning redundancy into an opportunity to explore the many possibilities that are available today. For example, further education could lead to new career paths. A job in a different sector may provide more security and even better benefits. Becoming your own boss may fulfil a long-cherished dream. Working from home may provide a more family-friendly lifestyle. List out the possibilities and consider them before dismissing them too quickly. Later chapters in this book provide useful guidance on the various options open to you.

Rising above redundancy and seeing it as a challenge to be overcome and not a setback to endure is a much more positive way to begin the process of moving on. Even the fact of moving to a new employer with hopefully better prospects and conditions can be an uplifting experience. There are many examples of people who, following redundancy, started their own businesses and are now running thriving companies. One individual turned his love of gardening into a successful landscape business; another turned her interest in fashion into a dressmaking enterprise. Many of these people will say that redundancy was one of the best things that ever happened to them, though perhaps it did not seem so when they first heard about it. Others have returned to further education or training which was not available to them in early life. They are now on new career paths that offer much greater potential and personal satisfaction.

Case Example 1

John had worked in information technology for seven years, first as a trainee programmer and later in maintenance of computer systems. His company decided to make the IT section in which he worked redundant and he was offered a package.

He had spotted what he thought was an opportunity to develop a software package to handle maintenance issues. However, he recognised that he had very little commercial experience. To make the venture work, he needed to team up with someone. He knew an individual in computer sales whom he liked and who seemed to have good commercial sense. Having discussed the idea with him, they decided to undertake a feasibility study with assistance from an Enterprise Ireland grant. The feasibility study suggested that a market existed both here and abroad but that considerable funding was required to develop the project commercially.

He went to Enterprise Ireland and got a grant towards the cost of undertaking the research and development. With this grant, as well as his redundancy payment, rebate of tax and some equity from his new partner, a software package was developed and tested successfully in the marketplace. His new venture was launched. In the early stages, contract systems maintenance work was taken on to augment the cash flow of the company. The company now has an office in Ireland and another in the UK and employs twenty-two people.

First actions on learning about redundancy

We briefly dealt earlier with the need to understand redundancy and the reasons for redundancy. Getting the facts clear will prevent you making erroneous decisions. It will also provide a better understanding and enable you to come to terms with your predicament. Remember, you are entitled to clear information about what is facing you, so do not be shy about asking questions. This is all new to you. No one can expect you to know and understand everything at first. There is a lot to absorb. Take one thing at a time and try to get as full an understanding as possible.

The following list of questions will enable you obtain a complete picture of the immediate implications of the redundancy:

1. Who exactly will be affected?

2. Is it voluntary or involuntary redundancy?

3. When precisely will it occur?

4. How will people be selected?

5. What terms are offered?

6. How much will the package be worth?

7. Are there different terms for different categories of employee?

8. Are there tax implications?

9. Will health and other insurance be paid up to date and beyond?

10. What will happen to my pension contributions?

11. What is the status of my pension?

12. Will my pension be frozen? Can I take it with me?

13. With whom can I discuss the status of my pension?

14. Are there options such as early retirement available?

15. Is there any room for negotiation in relation to the make up of the package?

16. If the business is not closing, where and how will the work I am currently doing be accomplished?

17. If it is to be outsourced, who will be undertaking it?

18. Are there opportunities for contracting back?

19. What are my social welfare entitlements?

20. Will the company provide support through the transition and, if so, in what form?

21. Will there be independent advice made available?

22. Will the company be giving references?

Relying on the grapevine for information about the impending redundancy is often a foolhardy business. It is necessary to get the facts directly from the source. Support from colleagues, or from your union if you are a member, is vital if you encounter difficulties. Write down all the facts about the redundancy, such as when it is going to happen, the payments and the options given, and make sure you fully understand what they mean. Confusion can reign at this stage, particularly if you are in an emotional state. Take advice on what options are available. Where the company is providing advice and support, take full advantage of its resources, particularly if the person giving the advice is both competent and impartial. If not, seek outside advice. Sources of advice include a respected and trusted individual you know, a solicitor or an accountant, a human resource manager from another organisation, a union official, FÁS or one of the many advice centres that are established in most towns and cities. Your local library or job centre will furnish you with their details.

Before dealing with any lump sum offered, you should find out all you can about the options for investing it wisely (see Chapter 3).

Access to a computer

One action that is recommended very early on is to get access to a computer with an internet facility. If you are lucky enough to have your own computer, you are at a distinct advantage. However, do not worry if you do not have a computer: you may be able to avail of facilities from your employer; local libraries, advice centres and even 'internet cafés' also provide internet access.

If you are unfamiliar with computers, do not be put off – they are not magic but they can be a powerful help to you. They can save hours finding out what you need to know at this critical stage in your work life. Advice centres usually have people who know exactly what to do and will gladly give you all the help that you need. You also probably know a friend or relative who has internet access and knowledge in this area. Often, a son or daughter, nephew or niece will be very familiar with using the computer for all sorts of activities. Avail of their expertise! You can reward them later with a gift for any help they give. Do not be shy about asking for help. Most people will understand perfectly and will be happy to come to your assistance.

It is important to gain access, directly or indirectly, to a computer for several reasons. Firstly, all the relevant support agencies have websites. These cover areas such as advice on social welfare entitlements, your legal and tax position, job opportunities, assistance for starting up your own business, educational opportunities, dealing with money matters and so on. Secondly, you can access organisations such as the Irish Organisation for the Unemployed that provide excellent support and advice on relevant matters ranging from entitlements to getting back to work. Thirdly, the internet has many sources of information on items from preparing a winning CV to ways of seeking the right career opportunities. Fourthly, most companies have websites that provide practical and useful information, enabling you to be well prepared for interviews or even to customise your CV to better suit the prospective employer's requirements. Finally, online job searching will give you wider access to job opportunities that otherwise might not be available to you.

The information and support is there to help you. Availing of it is essential, so do not be put off by any fears you may have in relation to computers.

Case Example 2

Joe worked for an engineering company as a fitter. The company was facing major competition and was coming under pressure to reduce costs. Management decided to cut the number of staff and reorganise the operations. They announced a voluntary redundancy programme but the terms did not attract sufficient volunteers. Much against the protestations of the union, they set about selecting individuals and drew up a list of names. No criteria were stated as to why particular individuals were selected. Much to Joe's shock and horror, his name was on the list. He felt that he had worked hard for the company and did everything that was asked of him. A few years ago, he had some problems with timekeeping but that was long behind him.

After overcoming the initial shock, he became quite angry. But he knew he had to calm down and do something about what he felt was very unfair. He confronted his manager and asked for an explanation as to why he was selected. He had been with the company longer than many who were not on the list. The manager talked about competition and briefly mentioned skills. Joe was unaware of any difficulty about his skills and felt the decision was made for other reasons, more to do with favouritism.

The redundancy package offered was poor and he knew that it would not last long, since he had a mortgage and a family to support. He approached his union and, with their help, he appealed the decision to the Employment Appeals Tribunal (EAT). He won his case and was offered the alternative of his job back or compensation. After some reflection, he felt he would not be happy working for that company again and so he decided to accept the compensation.

While the compensation package was good, Joe was anxious to get back to work and applied for a number of jobs locally. After a number of weeks, he obtained a job as a fitter in another company.

After five years, he was promoted to foreman. Joe went through a very difficult time for a period but he was proud that he stood up for himself and that he was vindicated by the EAT.

CHAPTER 3

Redundancy – The Legal, Social Welfare and Tax Aspects

Many people who are made redundant consider themselves completely cut loose. Yet this is not quite the case. Employers still have to meet certain obligations to you in order to assist you through the transition.

When considering your rights, firstly, look at the legal definition of redundancy and make sure it is consistent with your dismissal. Secondly, examine your contract of employment and any specific provisions contained therein. Thirdly, if there is a company-wide agreement, examine the provisions negotiated and contained in it. While this may not be legally enforceable in all circumstances, there will at least be a moral obligation on the employer to comply with them. These three elements will be important. In unionised employments, they will be likely taken up by the union official as bases for negotiating final terms and conditions.

Notice obligations

The employer must provide proper notification to the Department of Enterprise, Trade and Employment. If a number of people are being made redundant under the criteria stated below, thirty days' notice must be given to the Minister for Enterprise, Trade and Employment. This applies if

- 5 people are being made redundant when the business employs more than 20 employees and less than 50

- 10 employees are being let go when the business employs more than 50 and less than 100 employees

- 10 per cent of employees are being let go when the business employs at least 100 but less than 300 employees.

These obligations are imposed on employers by law, which also provides direct safeguards for those who are made redundant.

Contractual notice

The employee's employment contract must be examined in order to determine precisely your notice entitlement. If there is no such entitlement stated on the contract, then the employee is entitled by law to certain minimum periods of notice. If you have been employed with the company for between:

- 13 weeks and 2 years, you are entitled to at least 1 week's notice

- 2 and 5 years, you are entitled to 2 weeks' notice

- 5 and 10 years, you are entitled to 4 weeks' notice

- 10 and 15 years, you are entitled to a minimum of 6 weeks' notice.

Fair selection

Those selected to be made redundant must be selected on grounds that are fair and without prejudice. For the redundancy to be fair there are a number of criteria that the employer has to meet in accordance with the law. For example, under the Employment Equality Act, 1998, it is prohibited under law for an individual to be selected for redundancy solely on the grounds of gender, age, marital status, family status, race, religious beliefs, membership of the travelling community, disability and sexual orientation.

The employer has responsibility to prove that the individual selected for redundancy was selected without bias and completely objectively. The grounds or criteria on which the selection takes place must be made clear and communicated to the employee. If this has not been done, then clarification should be sought.

Redundancy payments

The Redundancy Payments Acts, 1967–2003 oblige employers by law to pay redundant employees what is known as 'statutory redundancy entitlement'. This amount is related to the employee's length of service and normal weekly earnings: the total of gross weekly wage, average regular overtime and payment-in-kind, up to a maximum at 2004 of €600.00 per week.

Exactly who is covered?

- An employee between the ages of 16 and 66 (old age pension age)

- An employee with 104 weeks' (two years') continuous service

- An employee who is insurable for all benefits under the Social Welfare Acts and is normally expected to work for 18 hours or more per week

- Part-time workers with less than 18 hours per week do not have to be fully insurable but must satisfy the rest of the conditions.

Employers who pay the statutory redundancy entitlement and give proper notice of redundancy (at least two weeks) are entitled to a 60 per cent refund from the Social Insurance Fund, into which they make regular payments themselves through PRSI contributions.

What happens if an employer is unable to pay a redundancy lump sum?

Employers are obliged to make redundancy payments in accordance with the statutory requirements laid down under the Redundancy Payments Acts. In situations where the employer is unable to pay the employees their entitlements, the Department of Enterprise, Trade and Employment pays the full amount direct to the employees from the Social Insurance Fund (SIF). The employee sends in Form RP 14 (see next section on redundancy forms). The Department usually treats these applications as a priority and later seeks reimbursement from the employer via its Redundancy Recoveries Section.

How is the lump sum calculated?

➢ Two weeks' pay for each year of continuous and reckonable employment between the ages of 16 and 66 years:

- In addition, a bonus week
- Reckonable service is service excluding ordinary sick-leave over and above 26 weeks, occupational injury over and above 52 weeks, maternity leave over 18 weeks and career breaks over 13 weeks in a 52-week period
- Reckonable service does not include absence from work because of lay-offs or strikes; however, short-time work is reckonable

➢ All calculations are subject to the ceiling referred to above, which at 2004 stands at €600.00 per week.

Please note that you can now check your own calculation at the online redundancy calculator www.redcalc.entemp.ie

Redundancy forms

There are a range of forms associated with redundancy used by the Department of Enterprise, Trade and Employment and these are listed below.

For completion by the employer:

- *RP1* – Notice of Redundancy – employees with two years' service must get at least two weeks' notice, gradually rising to eight weeks with at least fifteen years' service. A copy of the form must be sent to the Department.

- *RP2* – Certificate of Redundancy – contains the figures used to calculate the redundancy lump sum, for example number of years' service reckonable for redundancy purposes, weekly pay and so on. It must be signed by both the employer and employee. No alteration should be made to the form once it has been signed.

- *RP3* – Claim for Rebate – submitted by the company and must be sent to the Department within six months of payment of redundancy.

For completion by the employee:

- *RP6* – Where employee proposes to leave before the expiry of the date of termination of redundancy – employer's consent required.

- *RP14* – Employee's Application for Redundancy Payment from the Social Insurance Fund, where employer fails to pay redundancy payment. This form must be accompanied by form RP1 and either a completed Redundancy Certificate (RP2) or a copy of a favourable decision from the Employment Appeals Tribunal (EAT).

Right of redress

There is a considerable body of case law and precedents that qualifies and adds to the statutory provisions mentioned already. Expert advice from a solicitor or trade union may be necessary. In the event that you think you have been unfairly selected or have not received your statutory entitlement, disputes concerning redundancy payments can be submitted to the EAT, which has the advantage of providing a speedy, fair, inexpensive and informal means for individuals to seek remedies for alleged infringements of their statutory redundancy rights. The EAT deals with disputes under such other labour law areas as the Minimum Notice and Terms of Employment Acts, 1973–2001. These Acts cover the right of workers to a minimum period of notice before dismissal, provided they have been in continuous service with the same employer for at least 13 weeks and are normally expected to work at least 8 hours per week. The EAT also deals with the Unfair Dismissals Acts, 1977–1993 and, where the employer is insolvent, the Protection of Employees (Employers' Insolvency) Acts, 1984–2003, which deal with such areas as arrears of pay due to an employee, holiday and sick pay etc.

Case Example 3

Willie had worked hard and had risen over the past ten years through the ranks to become production manager in a subsidiary of a multinational company. He had qualified as production engineer and attended a number of short courses on management. The company decided to close the subsidiary and he was made redundant. While he had been aware that this was a possibility for some time, it still left him in a state of shock when it happened.

He received a reasonable redundancy package and pondered what he would do next. He had the possibility of getting similar jobs locally but felt they offered little prospect for progression. He was anxious to progress his career. He had enjoyed his management role and the management courses he had attended. A number of his friends had completed a Masters of Business Administration (MBA) course and, having discussed with them what the course covered, Willie felt that it would suit him. He had the option of doing the course on a part-time or full-time basis. He sat down with his partner and discussed the options. With some sacrifices, he would be able to do the course full time and concluded that this was the best option.

He completed his MBA and as the end of the course approached, he began applying for positions. One of the companies he applied to was a management consultancy specialising in advising manufacturing companies on how to improve their processes. He accepted a position with them. After three years, he was offered the position of general manager with a growing company and now happily operates in that capacity. Whether he would have taken this course of action if he had not been made redundant is debatable. He thinks probably not. No matter, he turned redundancy into a positive career progression.

Social welfare entitlements

When redundancy occurs, there are social welfare benefits you can look forward to receiving. This can be a complicated area for those not familiar with it. Booklets and leaflets are available from the Department of Social and Family Affairs and they also have a very comprehensive website. In addition, local social welfare offices and Citizen Information Centres will provide advice and information.

It is useful to know the difference between Unemployment Benefit and Unemployment Assistance. Broadly speaking, the difference between the two is that to receive Unemployment Benefit, you must have contributed PRSI previously while working and, now that you are unemployed, you are entitled to benefits based on these contributions. Unemployment Assistance is a modest level of means-tested support guaranteed by the state, irrespective of previous employment.

To qualify for Unemployment Benefit, you must be:

- Aged sixteen or over
- Unemployed for at least three days out of any six
- Available for full-time work
- Capable of full-time work
- Genuinely seeking full-time work.

Unemployment Benefit is taken from an individual's PRSI contribution record or 'stamps'. You will need to have paid thirty-nine contributions since you began work and thirty-nine contributions within the governing contribution year. The governing contribution year is throughout the tax year before the claim. If you have used up your Unemployment Benefit, you need to work and pay thirteen contributions before you can claim a new Unemployment Benefit payment.

Since the recent budget (2004), certain allowances such as widow's or widower's contributory and non-contributory pensions may affect the payments you receive. Some of these changes have been rescinded since the budget, so it would be wise to check with the local welfare office as regards the current position. No increase is made for child dependants.

Unemployment Assistance is a means-tested social welfare payment for those who do not have enough PRSI contributions to claim Unemployment Benefit and are eighteen years or over.

The following are included for means testing:

- Cash income, including income earned by spouses, occupational pensions and renting out a room in your home
- The value of any property you own, except the home you live in
- Investments, savings and capital
- The value of benefit and privilege arising from food and lodging in parents' home.

You must provide information on any of the items you listed above when asked or your claim may be delayed or refused.

What do you need in order to claim an unemployment payment?

- A P45 or a letter from your employer saying when you finished work

- A letter from your employer indicating that you finished work through no fault of your own may help speed up your claim

- Your long-form birth certificate

- Proof of your address (ESB bill, phone bill, etc.)

- For Unemployment Benefit, you need the record of your earnings in the relevant tax year – in other words your P60

- Proof that you are seeking full-time employment; you will be asked what sort of work you are looking for and what hours you are available to work – if possible be flexible

- You must show that you are looking for full-time employment and are willing to except any reasonable offer of employment

- If you have any children you may be asked what child-minding arrangements you have in place, as you must show you can take up work at short notice

- Proof that you are registered with FÁS.

Interim payments

While you are waiting for your claim to be decided, you could possibly be entitled to an interim payment or an exceptional or 'urgent needs payment' from the health board. Ask about this in the Employment Exchange when you are claiming Unemployment Benefit.

Withdrawal of an unemployment payment

You can lose your entitlement to an unemployment payment if:

- You refuse a suitable job offer, including community employment or a suitable FÁS course

- You are suspected or convicted of fraud in relation to a social welfare payment.

You must also inform the social welfare office of any change in your circumstances. Specifically, you must inform them if:

• You take up voluntary work

• You receive any other benefit or assistance

• You return to education

• You leave the country

• You become unable to take up employment

• Your family circumstances change.

Remember, to qualify for an unemployment payment you must be genuinely seeking, available for and capable of full-time employment. It is important to keep a record of all attempts you have made to find employment. Get a folder and in it file notes on all the phone calls you have made and copies of letters you have sent, job advertisements that you have answered and letters from employers.

Under the rules of the national Employment Action Plan (EAP), you may be called for an interview, where you may be offered a number of options, usually employment or education, or you may be referred to the Local Employment Service for more intensive guidance.

You may wish to note that under the EAP:

• The Department of Social Family Affairs writes to each person on the live register at the six/nine month unemployment threshold, informing them of the time of their interview with FÁS

• FÁS will inform the Department if you fail to attend the interview but will take no action themselves; the Department could require you to attend the interview in the local labour exchange

• Your payment may be cut off if you can give no reasonable explanation for not attending the FÁS interview

• If you appear at the interview but do not take up the option which is offered to you, FÁS will inform the Department through its regular tracking reports

• The Department may decide to interview you themselves to determine the result of your failure to take up the option offered to you.

The rules above may seem very fussy but, fundamentally, they are there to help you.

The facilities on offer could help you get back on your feet. You may have no need to resort to the recourse stated above but it is good to know that there is assistance on offer if you need it.

Taxation on redundancy payments

Generally speaking, all payments made by employers to employees and directors are regarded as 'pay' for tax purposes. Lump-sum payments on a redundancy or a retirement, however, qualify for special treatment and may be exempt or at least qualify for some relief.

Tax exemption is allowed if:

1. It is a statutory redundancy payment

2. The employment consisted of foreign service and certain conditions are met – more information on this is available from the Revenue Commissioners.

Lump-sum payments that qualify for some relief are:

*   **Salary or wages in lieu of notice**. However, where the contract of employment provides for a payment of this kind on termination of the contract, such payment is chargeable to tax in the normal way.

*   **Non-statutory redundancy payment**, i.e. amount given by your employer that is above that given as a statutory payment. If your employer gives all or part of the lump sum in some other form, such as a car, the equivalent cash value of the item received is taxable.

It can be a little complicated to calculate but the following are the rules currently prevailing. As of 2003, €10,158 of any other redundancy payment is not liable to tax. This minimum amount is increased by €762 for each full year of service with your employer. Any refund of pension contributions made by you is treated separately and taxed at the 20 per cent rate.

Basic exemption

In order to determine the actual exemption, we must bear in

mind the figure of €10,158 plus €765 for each full year of service. The figure is reduced by the amount of any other tax-free payments but will not be reduced below the minimum level of €10,158.

Example

Joe receives €16,000 as a redundancy lump sum after 10 years' service.

The basic exemption due to him is €10,158 plus €765 x 10, making it €17,808.

There is no tax payable as the lump sum of €16,000 is less than the €17,808 allowable.

Increased exemption

If you are not a member of an occupational pension scheme or if you have irrevocably given up your right to receive a lump sum from the pension scheme, then the basic exemption is increased by a further €10,000. The increased exemption can only be claimed if you have not made any claims in respect of a lump sum received in the previous ten tax years. In the case of the example above, the exemption level would rise to €27,808, assuming no previous claims were made.

Standard Capital Superannuation Benefit

For those with long service, there is a better option of going for what is known as the Standard Capital Superannuation Benefit (SCSB). SCSB is a relief given for each year of service equal to one-fifteenth of the average annual pay for the last three years of service.

The calculation is as follows:

$$AS \times N/15 \text{ less } PS$$

Where

AS = average salary over the past three years

N = the number of complete years' service

PS = any tax-free lump sum paid or due from a pension scheme

Example

Phil has 20 years' service and his total pay for the previous 36 months was €90,000. His redundancy package includes the following:

- Non-statutory redundancy   €40,000
- Statutory redundancy   €12,000
- Pay in lieu of notice   €1,000
- Company car valued at €4,000   €4,000
- Tax free lump sum from pension fund   €7,000

Statutory redundancy is tax exempt and is therefore ignored in the calculation.

Total lump sum is therefore €40,000 + €1,000 + €4,000 = €45,000

Basic exemption = €10,158 + €765 x 20 = €25,458

Increased exemption = €10,158 + €765 x 20 + €3,000 (the difference between the €10,000 allowance and the lump sum from the pension fund of €7,000)

This equals €28,458 of a tax-free allowance or €3,000 over the basic exemption allowance. Using the Standard Capital Superannuation Benefit (SCSB) calculation
SP = 7,000
N = 20
AS = 90,000/3
SCSB = 90,000/3 x 20/15 – 7,000 = €40,000

The highest exemption is the SCSB at €40,000, as it is greater than the €28,458. This is the option Phil should select.

Tax would be charged on €5,000 (€45,000 – €40,000).

The basic exemption and the SCSB are generally available against any subsequent lump-sum payment, provided the employer is not the same one or an associated employer. If, however, you have received a lump sum in the previous five years and availed of tax relief, then you may find that this tax relief will be deducted by the amount of relief already given.

It is possible to shelter part, or all, of a redundancy lump sum by using it to make additional voluntary contributions to a pension scheme. There are limits on the amount you can put in, but these are reasonably generous. The disadvantage of making extra contributions into the pension scheme is that the money cannot be accessed before retirement.

Which method is best depends on the individual's circumstances. If in doubt, it is best to take advice either from a tax adviser or by contacting your local tax office directly. The rate of tax applying to your lump sum will be that which you are currently paying. In certain circumstances, you may be able to avail of additional relief known as 'top slicing'. Top slicing relief relates to the rate at which you pay tax after exemptions mentioned above. It ensures that your lump sum is not taxed at a rate that is higher than the average rate you were taxed at for the five years prior to redundancy.

The formula that is applied is as follows:

Taxable lump sum x (tax rate applied to lump sum – average tax rate for previous five years)

If you are married, the joint income of yourself and your spouse is taken into account in calculating the taxes. It is claimed after the year-end.

Example

Fred was made redundant and had a taxable lump sum of €10,000. This is taxed at his marginal rate of 42%. His average rate of tax over the past five years was 38%.

Top slicing relief = €10,000 x (42% – 38%) = €400

The tax payable by Fred is reduced by a further €400.

Case Example 4

Stephen was made redundant after five years working as a sales clerk. His notice of redundancy was received suddenly. Apparently, it had been decided behind closed doors. He and ten other sales clerks were to be let go. Although different rumours had abounded throughout the firm, he had dismissed them, as he had been a good, conscientious worker. He had absolutely no inkling that he would be one of the victims.

At first, when he heard the news, he was angry and belligerent. The finer points of the business economics of cutbacks meant nothing to him – just empty talk. The reality, as he saw it, was that he just was not wanted. Soon a mood of despondency set in. He and his fellow co-workers became thoroughly demoralised. Stephen felt inadequate and was unable to muster the energy even to apply for a new job. He was upset that he could not provide for his young family.

He contacted his local social welfare office and sought advice. He needed his dole payment to provide for himself and his family. To qualify for social welfare, the requirements were that he had to try to find a new job or apply for entry to a FÁS course. He went to his local FÁS centre and soon discovered that there were options for people in his situation – not just options, but opportunities to grow and be a success in his own right. He sought advice and decided to take the training. He became proficient in computers and found, despite himself, that he was enjoying this experience. The training was not like the dark days of school but was designed with adults in mind. Soon he had discovered he had a talent for computer programming. He applied for jobs as a computer programmer and, after a number of interviews, he was successful and progressed in his new company to become a project leader.

Often the barriers we experience in life are self-imposed. Stephen triumphed over his despondency by opening his mind to new possibilities. In hindsight, he was grateful he was made redundant – otherwise he would have missed the chance to progress.

CHAPTER 4

Assessing your own Situation

Having got a handle on what the company is offering in terms of payments and other benefits and what social welfare payments you are entitled to, you need to assess your own particular circumstances. Doing an audit of your own situation involves analysing two key areas:

1. Assessing your financial position

2. Assessing your capabilities/personal assets in terms of skills, experience, aptitudes and motivations.

Assessing your financial position

When faced with redundancy, most of your initial practical worries will be financial. You will need to know your exact financial position in order to find out what room you have to consider your options.

- What about the mortgage?

- Car loan?

- Holiday?

- Insurance premiums?

It will help if you tackle these worries immediately. You should address the following commitments:

- **Your mortgage** – explain what has happened to your lender immediately and listen to their advice. Make sure you understand the current mortgage position, what is out-standing and how long it has to go. If they are aware of your situation, they may be able to offer alternative arrangements. Make careful notes of their suggestions and how long any interim arrangement would last. Be careful about any re-mortgaging offers as these can be quite expensive in the long run.

- **Loans and credit cards** – explain your circumstances, as above. You may have taken out insurance protection against unemployment to cover these debts. If so, now is the time to contact the insurers. Make sure expensive credit such as credit cards are dealt with first. Establish clearly what is outstanding and what the repayment levels are. If you foresee any difficulties, contact your lender and discuss making alternative arrangements, perhaps suspending payments for a period or paying just the interest element.

- **Life and home insurance** – it is not advisable to stop paying premiums on these insurances. If payments are due, it may be possible to pay over an extended period. Contact the companies and find out what alternative arrangements can be made in the short term.

- **Private medical insurance** is in a different category because it is not essential, though currently it is quite important. If you wish to continue your payments, contact the company to ask how they can help you through this period.

- **Holidays** and other planned expenditure – you may be able to cancel or postpone these.

- List **other regular payments** such as heating and light, television licence, car insurance and tax, school fees.

- Calculate **outgoings** on groceries, petrol, clothing, entertainment and other household expenditures with a view to establishing a realistic budget within which you can work.

Assessing your outgoings in cash terms establishes a budget of current expenditures. There may be opportunities to curtail these for the time being, at least giving you extra breathing space. Involving your family in the process is vital and making sure they understand the situation will avoid needless conflict and misunderstanding. Being open and consulting with them, enlisting their support where possible, will give them a sense of inclusion and you a sense of support through what can be a very difficult time for everyone.

Regaining control is a priority. Facing up to the realities now and, if necessary, making difficult decisions will mean that you

Table 4.1: Weekly or Monthly Budget

Outgoings	Amount	Incoming Monies	Amount
Rent/mortgage			
Loans			
Credit cards			
Leases/rentals			
Insurance			
Groceries			
Hardware			
Petrol			
Tax			
TV licence			
School/college fees/books			
Clothes			
Light			
Central heating			
Telephone			
Memberships			
Papers			
Entertainment			
Transport			
		Social welfare	
		Interest	
		Children's allowance	
		Other	
Total	€	€	€
Difference			€

regain control, which will give you the confidence to move on. Going into self-denial or avoiding issues can make matters worse, ultimately leaving you with less control and fewer options.

Getting a clear idea of your financial position and any redundancy payments on offer means you can consider what opportunities you can pursue and how much time you have to explore them. If your financial position is weak, you may feel the need to take any reasonable offer of employment – part-

time or otherwise that you can get. This may not be as good a
course of action to achieve your long-term goals as waiting for
the right job opportunity to come along which would further
your career much more. Though, as is said, 'any port in a storm
is better than being shipwrecked at sea'.

Investing the lump sum

If you have been fortunate enough to get a decent lump sum
from your redundancy, then you have to make a decision as to
what is the best way to get the most out of it. Of course, you
may want to spend some of it on necessary household repairs
or other areas such as undertaking a course or providing for a
child's education. Alternatively, you may want to pay off some
of your loans.

In general terms, if you are paying a higher rate on a loan
than you can get from investing the lump sum, then the sensible
thing to do is to pay off the loan. Early repayment on some
loans may incur penalties, so check out the position before
making any decision. If you have a mortgage on which you are
getting tax relief or if you have a loan with a very low interest
rate, then it may not make sense to pay off the loan or mortgage,
particularly if you plan to borrow in the future when it might
not be possible to get such good value.

You may also have decided you want to establish your own
business. In this event, you will likely need at least part of the
lump sum as equity.

Where none of the above options applies, then you have a
number of alternative ways of investing your monies. The first
thing to do is establish your objectives. Normally, you want to
invest your lump sum where it will give the best return after tax
with an acceptable level of risk. Here are some of the options
that are worth considering.

Deposit accounts

The current rate of return is very low. The rate you get is also
dependent on how long you can leave your money on deposit.
Shopping around to get the best rate is worthwhile.

Post-office accounts

These are not offering much of a return at present but they offer a high level of security.

With profit bonds

These are bonds offered by insurance companies that generally guarantee the return of the capital after a fixed period. The period can be as short as five years. Annual bonuses, although not guaranteed, are paid on the capital sum and there is a hope of a terminal bonus at the end of the investment term.

Rates are currently at 4 or 5 per cent but recent stock market fluctuations have put a question mark over their ability to continue at these levels. Whether the stock markets recover enough is still uncertain.

Investment funds

These funds can offer long-term growth. Risks associated with them vary depending on the fund chosen. Some will offer guarantees such as tracker bonds that follow specified stock-market indices. Returns have been good recently with the recovery in the stock market.

Property

Property has been an attractive investment over the past number of years, though whether this will continue is anyone's guess – even economists differ on the prospects for the future. Also, unless the lump sum is really substantial, then it is unlikely you will be able to afford such an investment.

Tax-based schemes

Tax relief is available on some property investments. Investing in expanding manufacturing, international traded service companies, certain music ventures and tourism can achieve significant tax relief but also can be highly risky and should really only be undertaken when the monies put in are not depended upon for the future.

Shares

Shares can provide a good return if you know what you are doing and you are lucky. The more you know what you are doing, the luckier you are likely to be. Unfortunately, there are no guarantees. Over the longer term, shares have tended to rise faster than inflation and have the advantage that most pay both dividends and offer capital growth. Selecting the right ones, keeping a close eye on the company and trading at the right time, particularly after a period of high performance, are some of the secrets of success.

Annuities

You purchase these from an insurance company that, in turn, promises to pay you an income for life. They tend to suit people as they get older. However, when you buy them, you are locked in for life. With interest rates currently low, the returns are also low. The longer you live, the better your return.

Getting Advice

When investing your monies, you are wise to take advice, ideally from more than one source. There are three types of advisers authorised by the Central Bank: single agency, multi-agency and authorised.

Single agency

These only work or hold an agency for one supplier and therefore will try to sell the offerings of that provider. In some cases, the offering may not be the best one or the one that suits your particular circumstances.

Multi-agency

These can offer products from a number of providers, though the number in many cases may be small. They are in a position to offer you a wider range of products but not in all cases will you get what is best for you.

Authorised

These are independent of all the institutions that supply investment products and they are expected to search the market for the very best offering that suits you. Naturally, they may be sometimes influenced by the levels of commission offered by the institutions, so do make sure you ask all the questions to satisfy yourself that you are actually getting the best deal.

Knowing what you want and your current financial position is a big help before sitting down with your adviser. Make sure that any of the pros and cons of each option are explained fully. Before you make a final decision, take time to consider all the angles and do not be rushed. A little time now can save heartache later on.

Assessing your capabilities

When assessing your own capabilities, remember to take as broad a perspective as possible while remaining realistic. It is far better if you take time out to examine in some detail what options are possible at this stage. Getting help to do this is advisable. It can be quite difficult to make an objective assessment of yourself. You may not appreciate fully your abilities or you may overestimate others. Adopting a systematic approach can make the process easier.

Start by looking at what skills you have, how these skills can be adapted to potential new situations or, as the case may be, how you can upgrade them or acquire new skills. Broadly speaking, there are four types of skills: basic, personal, job specific and transferable.

Basic skills

These are the fundamental skills that you use in everyday life, such as organising your life on a day-to-day basis and communicating with those around you. Other skills such as counting, writing or the ability to self-motivate can be included in this category also.

Personal skills

This is a wide category of skills, encompassing your attitudes and behaviour. These skills can affect everything from the way in which you communicate with others to the way in which you organise your professional life. Qualities such as enthusiasm, the ability to listen and good humour are of increasing appeal to employers.

Personal skills enable you to deploy all the other technical and vocational skills that are referred to below. For instance, it would be impossible to engage successfully in business negotiations without a flexible attitude and a good manner.

Writing down the skills you possess will give you a clearer picture of what your options are. Many people are surprised at the list they generate. Whether your list is long or short, always remember you have the ability to gain new skills and strengths if you so desire.

Job-specific skills

These are the skills that you have acquired at work or in education and may include craft skills, machine operation, driving and so on. Ability to understand and operate quality control systems, undertake stock checks, manage documentation and compile reports are just a few of the skills that can be considered under this heading. If you had a job specification in your former employment, it may help you to list these skills.

Transferable skills

Transferable skills are those we possess that are useful across a large number of disciplines, if not all vocations. For example, IT skills are a benefit in a wide range of jobs; leadership and linguistic skills could be beneficial in many businesses. Project management, presentation, analytical and problem-solving skills are other examples of transferable skills. You may have experience of coaching and mentoring, some of which you may have derived from your recreational pursuits. Do not forget these when making your assessment. Skills associated with working in a team environment and achieving results are increasingly sought by employers in today's work environment.

Table 4.2: Skills Self-Assessment*

Skill Area	Skill Description	Priority Listing (based on strength and personal satisfaction)
Basic 1. 2. 3. 4. 5. 6.		
Personal 1. 2. 3. 4. 5. 6.		
Job Specific 1. 2. 3. 4. 5. 6.		
Transferable 1. 2. 3. 4. 5. 6.		

*When filling out the table, brainstorm initially and then make a priority listing based on your strongest skills and what gives you the most satisfaction.

Under some of the headings, you may not be able to list six skills while under others, you may be able to list more. So be flexible as regards the number. Having completed the exercise above and given some thought to how your profile looks, you should discuss it with someone you trust to clarify your own assessment. This will help point you towards the best way forward.

Progressive companies may assist you by funding aptitude and personality tests, of which you should avail. The better picture you have of yourself, the better decision you can make about where you can focus and direct your efforts when moving on in your career.

Arriving at a decision

Now that you have completed your assessment of your financial position and your own capabilities, you have a number of options open to you. These range from:

• Seeking a similar position in another company

• Taking time out and building skills with additional training

• Moving into education on a part-time or full-time basis

• Starting your own business

• Changing your career

• Looking at part-time or home-based jobs

• Contracting your services.

Along with your assessment of your financial and personal capabilities, a number of other factors will also come into play now. For example, seeking a similar position in another company may mean relocating. This will have an obvious impact on spouses and children. In other situations, part-time working may be a paramount consideration if childcare is a major issue. Your personal ambitions may lead you in one particular direction and will override such matters as job security or even income potential.

It is often useful to discuss with a partner or trusted friend a wide range of scenarios clearly describing each course of action, what the likely outcomes are and what the impact will be on you and your family. In addition, writing down these scenarios provides a record of your thoughts, facilitates comparison and enables them to be revisited and considered after a period has elapsed.

Depending on the outcome of your assessment, one option will likely appear preferable to the others. Be careful not to close off options too early, as this may limit your flexibility; be wary of following too many, as this will dissipate your energies and focus. It is best to prioritise them in terms of preference and suitability.

Case Example 5

Bill had worked for the same company for over twenty years as a general operative when closure was announced. While he was shocked and dismayed, he began to think about his situation further.

He was in his late forties and had been unhappy with the job for some time. His wages were not great and changes in work practices meant his job gave little or no satisfaction. He received statutory redundancy. While the sum was small, it was sufficient for him to consider his options. The building industry was booming around his area and he fancied the idea of working in it. He talked to a number of people and, provided he obtained basic training, a position would be available to him. He registered with FÁS and undertook training as a construction plant operator. This enabled him to get a job in the building industry. Although the work was more demanding, doing something he enjoyed at a higher wage level made up for this.

CHAPTER 5

Types of Careers

The changing concept of work

The concept of work is changing. The psychological contract under which employees strived for the organisation and the organisation was expected to look out for their best interests no longer prevails. Legal enforcement of certain basic requirements in terms of duty of care exists, but old loyalties are fading.

Similarly, employees are becoming more individualistic and looking out for their own interests, including job satisfaction and a high level of income. They have a growing concern for leisure and family pursuits and no longer see their job as their main life focus. New career and job opportunities are emerging with different contractual arrangements.

In seeking out a new career and work life, it is worthwhile being aware of these trends and using this enforced break to take a broader perspective of work and consider how you can capitalise on emerging trends.

Let us examine some of these trends:

- The number of permanent, pensionable jobs is decreasing. Contracting for fixed periods is increasing, as is part-time employment

- Outsourcing of non-core activities by companies and the public sector is growing in areas such as accounting, payroll and personnel, maintenance, security, catering, cleaning and so on

- Multiple-skilling and/or cross-skilling are becoming the norm – this is most obvious with craftsmen becoming technicians and machine operators becoming process operators

- The level of educational requirements is rising and qualifications are now becoming the minimum for more and more jobs

- Service-sector jobs are rising while manufacturing and agricultural jobs are, if anything, declining

- Working from home, while relatively slow to take off in Ireland, is growing and the speed of growth will likely increase in the future with the development of new technology and broadband.

These trends will have a major impact on job seekers and the nature of job opportunities in the future. For employees to meet these new trends, they will require:

- Adaptability to new circumstances

- Continuing education and skills acquisition leading to specific qualifications

- Enhanced IT skills and access to computer facilities

- Flexible and portable pensions

- Self-reliance

- Commercial awareness and management skills

- Abilities in terms of negotiation and self-management.

Where will the new opportunities likely emerge?

Service-based sectors such as maintenance, catering and hospitality, leisure, entertainment, event management, hygiene, landscaping, health care and retailing are growing. *Knowledge-based sectors* such as computer software, education, technical and industrial design, medical, pharmaceutical and bio-technology are also growing.

Assessing the opportunities

Moving on in your career is not just a short-term decision; it sets the path for the medium term. Obviously, depending on your circumstances, there may not be much opportunity to be selective. However, it would be foolish not to be aware of the changing environment and risk suffering the same fate again.

In planning your move forward, there is a range of questions that you should ask:

- Is the sector I am considering growing or declining?

- What new trends are emerging in terms of technology, new competitors, outsourcing, reward including pensions and so on?

- How am I geared to take advantage of these?

- How will these trends fit in with my ambitions, lifestyle and desires for the future?

- Are there mergers and acquisitions taking place and what will be their impact?

- Are there specific jobs or opportunities in the sector that are reasonably secure and becoming more important?

- Are there local opportunities or will I have to move?

- Does the sector provide career development including training and educational opportunities?

- Are new qualifications emerging that are needed if career progression is to take place?

- Would home-based working be available and would it be desirable or suitable?

- Does my experience and training offer the sector what it is looking for?

- Would it be better to take time out and acquire new qualifications?

- Are there opportunities to supply or contract services?

Depending on your answers to these questions, you will be able to decide on the broad direction you would like to go and at least not waste your time going down a cul-de-sac.

There is no doubt that there are more supports available now than ever to take a bold step forward to a new future and these will be explored later. To avail of these, awareness of their existence is obviously important. Even more important is confidence to set your goals and to go after them. After the shattering experience of redundancy, confidence may be low and there is a natural tendency to focus on our weaknesses rather than looking to our strengths. Now is the time to think about these strengths and use them to move forward.

Case Example 6

Geraldine had worked in a financial office for five years until it closed down and she was made redundant. She had gained a lot of experience of how business worked and of dealing with the public.

She often felt that she would like to work for herself. She was tired of commuting and wanted to work nearer to home, which was in the country. She was keenly interested in gardening – and flowers in particular. Her local village was growing rapidly and she felt that an opportunity existed to establish a flower shop there. With the help of a friend who was an accountant, they assessed what was involved in financial terms and put together a business plan. Her redundancy payment was small but together with a bank loan, she had enough to undertake the venture. When she approached the bank initially, they were reluctant to give her the loan. Fortunately, she had savings in the credit union and they agreed to give her the loan.

Getting the business established took a lot of effort and time. The first two years were hard and finance was very tight. However, the business gradually began to grow and is now thriving.

CHAPTER 6

Educational Opportunities

Exploring the options open to you

Being made redundant can give you a chance to think about whether you would like to change career, develop new skills, recharge the batteries and move on to pastures new. Now is your time to do this. You might feel you need to return to further education. There are now many opportunities for adults to undertake a range of courses and training programmes – from degree courses to acquiring basic skills. These are accessible to and inclusive of all.

The following are a few examples of what you might consider undertaking:

- Acquiring some computer skills

- Increasing your understanding of IT

- Developing supervisory skills

- Learning basic foreign language skills

- Developing your ability to communicate better.

These and more courses are available from The Vocational Education Committees (VECs), FÁS and the Institutes of Technology.

You may have been an experienced manager in one of the functional areas such as production or finance and you may want to develop a broader business perspective. There are advanced courses leading to degree and masters degree levels available from the Institutes of Technology and Universities. One of the main problems faced by potential participants is which one to choose!

Many people can be intimidated by the prospect of returning to further education, particularly if they have been away from formal education for a long time. Hours of boredom in school, stuck in classrooms, studying subjects in which they had no interest leaves its mark. It is hard to appreciate that learning in a classroom can actually be a fun as well as a rewarding experience. Adult learners enjoy advantages over young people. You will likely be studying something you are interested in and perhaps will already have experience related to the area and how the learning is applied in real life. This provides a motivation, which is very important to anyone undertaking any course.

It might be worth considering taking on a short course first to give you a taste of what it is like to resume education. These courses are designed in such a manner as to take full account of peoples' fears. The tutors also understand the different needs of adults and are trained to support participants, especially in the early stages. They appreciate that people may lack confidence and need time to adjust. Remember, the approach and environment in adult education is not at all similar to your old school days. The environment allows individuals to progress at their own rate. There will be support from other participants who are in a similar position if any difficulties arise.

Apart from the educational benefits, courses also provide a great opportunity to socialise and interact with other people who have similar concerns and worries. Lasting friendships are often formed.

What is available?

AONTAS is the Irish National Association of Adult Education. It has 484 statutory and voluntary members, all of which provide education opportunities. Community education has developed strongly in recent years and it is estimated that there are over 1,000 women's groups and a smaller number of men's groups providing learning and development opportunities to a diverse range of people.

FÁS alone provides some four hundred courses annually throughout the country. They have a range of online courses. If you have a computer, you can learn in your home environment and at your own pace. Checking out what FÁS has to offer is a worthwhile starting point. This can be done at any of their sixty offices around the country.

As mentioned earlier, VECs, which are responsible for vocational and community schools, are very big providers of education. They offer a wide range of full-time and part-time courses through their Vocational Training Opportunities Schemes (VTOS). These programmes are excellent for adults who need to return to full-time education without losing their social welfare benefits. You may also be able to avail of travel and meal allowances, free books and exemption from fees. Certain conditions apply to these schemes and your local social welfare office will furnish you with details of eligibility.

The types of courses available include a two-year Leaving Certificate course, fast track into new technology and more. VTOS participants may also enrol in Post-Leaving Certificate Courses (PLCs) or Further Education (FE) courses, subject to completing the Leaving Certificate or acquiring suitable work experience. These courses may be used as a ladder to progress into relevant courses at third level, particularly in the Institutes of Technology. Information on all these courses is available from your local VEC. A list of useful sources of information covering the range of courses is available at the end of the book.

Generally, mature applicants are assessed on grounds other than the Leaving Certificate results. Universities usually look for some evidence of ability to follow and benefit from the proposed study programme. The larger VECs also provide a guidance service to adults wishing to undertake courses and it is wise to avail of this service where possible.

Getting qualifications

Today, certificates of qualifications as evidence of your skills are sought by most employers. Therefore, it is useful to understand what sort of award or qualification you will receive on completion of the course you are considering undertaking. For instance, the Further Education and Training Awards Council provides a qualification commonly known as FETAC. Most PLCs and some courses provided by Bord Iascaigh Mhara (BIM), CERT, FÁS and Teagasc meet FETAC's requirements. The Central Applications Office (CAO) based in Athlone lists almost the full range of courses on their website (www.cao.ie).

Universities and Institutes of Technology are gearing up with more courses for adults. Many of these are in modular form which means you can graduate to certificate and then to diploma level, before moving on, if you wish, to degree level. Each of the colleges would be happy to provide information about what is covered in each course and where job opportunities exist when you are qualified. There are also private colleges offering a whole range of courses. These tend to be more expensive but should not be ruled out completely, as many specialise in courses not generally available elsewhere.

In addition to the VTOS, unemployed adults may be entitled to retain their benefits while attending a full-time third level course in a University, Institute of Technology or other third level institution.

For adult learners attending courses that are approved by the Department of Education and Science for the Higher Education Grants Scheme there are two principal forms of assistance:

• The Back to Education Allowance and

• The Higher Education Grant.

The Back to Education Allowance is an educational opportunities scheme for unemployed people, lone parents and people with disabilities who are getting certain payments from the Department of Social and Family Affairs. The Higher Education Grant is for mature students who are at least twenty-three years of age on 1 January of the year of entry or re-entry to an approved course of third-level education in an approved institution and is subject to a means test. Details of the Back to Education Allowance scheme are available from the local office of the Department of Social and Family Affairs. Details of the Higher Education Grants are available from the Department of Education and Science. A *Guide for Mature Students on Entry into Full-Time Third Level Courses* published by the Department of Education and Science is available free to any interested parties.

Education is now seen as a right for all and not just for the few. Availing of the opportunities out there is an investment in you. And there can be no better investment than an investment in you. Further education is a rewarding experience and will open doors to new opportunities, creating previously unreachable possibilities for the future. It will also help build your confidence, which may be flagging after redundancy.

Case Example 7

Mary was made redundant after working for thirteen years in assembly with an engineering company. The redundancy came as a shock. Apart from the loss of income, she would miss her workmates greatly. Fortunately, her partner had a job and was progressing well. Her two children were now at secondary school and no longer needed a child minder. She received a good redundancy package.

Mary had left school at Intermediate Certificate level, as it was known then. She attended night classes on computers in her local school and had enjoyed them. Pondering her situation, she felt the urge to move on. Little opportunity for similar employment existed locally anyway.

She decided to take a secretarial course in her local VEC. This was full time for one year. As she was finishing the course, an opportunity came up to work part time with a small local business in the reception area and carrying out some administrative duties and she took it. She got on well in her new position and picked up the office routines quickly, though at the beginning she had to work hard. Gradually, she was given new areas of responsibility and began attending night classes in accounts and office administration. The bookkeeper in the company left and she was promoted to this position and appointed office manager.

CHAPTER 7

Seeking another Position

Seeking out opportunities

You will have had time by now to reflect on your personal position and to consider what way you wish to progress your career. Deciding on your preferred choices will enable you to focus your job search.

The beginning of the search will involve preparing your CV and how to do this is covered in more detail in Chapter 8. Putting a lot of effort into preparing a good CV is worthwhile. The CV is the first point of contact with any prospective employer and initially the only means whereby you can be judged as being a suitable applicant for a position within the company. You will likely be amongst many who are seeking the position and, therefore, an initial screening process will be necessary. Whether or not you are called for interview by a prospective employer will depend on your CV.

Having prepared the best possible CV, you have to decide where to send it. The first targets will be FÁS and the recruitment agencies. You will have registered with FÁS anyway if you are claiming social welfare entitlements. Try to select recruitment agencies that specialise in your field, as these will understand you and know better what opportunities are available.

The second range of possibilities will be in response to advertised positions in the media and on websites. Do not forget to look up past editions of the newspaper as well as the current ones.

The third focus will be companies in the region or locality who may be recruiting candidates but who may not have advertised. Most people agree that the best jobs are never advertised but are filled by word of mouth.

Each of us has built up networks over the years, either through work or recreation and this can be a fourth option open to us. Simply put, networks are people we know who have a range of contacts with other people, some of whom might be useful in this situation. Contacting individuals in your networks who may be aware of companies with vacancies within their extended networks is a very powerful and often undervalued way of seeking out job opportunities. Many people feel shy about doing this but it is worthwhile overcoming this reserve, as the dividends can be high.

Of course, some companies may use 'outplacement' specialists to help you seek out opportunities. You would be wise to take full advantage of these. However, it would be wrong to place an over-reliance on them. A far more likely strategy for success is to remain proactive and in control of your own employment search.

One of the more modern ways to seek a position is to go online and to benefit from the incredible power of the internet. The internet can be used in three ways:

1. Creating information: creating CVs, covering letters, follow-up letters and so on

2. Gathering information: finding job openings and information about companies you might like to join – most significant companies have websites, which can be wonderful sources of information on the company that could take you weeks to find otherwise

3. Disseminating information: getting employers' attention with your CV and covering letter.

As time goes by, more people will use online job-hunting techniques. Anyone who takes advantage of it now will be in the forefront and may have an edge. Employers will likely be impressed with this approach and, because of this, more attention will be paid to you. It is easier for you to target the right companies and it is easier for companies to store and access your CV.

Traditional recruitment advertising is now moving online. While figures for Ireland are not available, over one million jobs in the UK are posted annually in what are known as job banks. Job banks list job vacancies, just as do newspapers. The big difference is that you do not have to go through all the applicants – using key words, the computer does that for you. FÁS operates such a job bank and there are also a number of private providers. This is covered in more detail in Chapter 8.

The internet also allows employers to find you in ways that were never available before. In the same way as there are job banks, there are also CV banks. Anyone can post their CV on a CV bank. The CV bank allows you to post your credentials and personal details anonymously for viewing by interested parties.

Increasingly, companies are storing CVs in electronic databases. This is true whether you send them to the company in hard copy or electronically. In practice, any recruiter can source thousands of CVs from their office, so it is important to understand how the system works (this is explained later). You can also search for companies you would like to join by looking up their websites or going through directories. This broadens your search base considerably. Unfortunately, many of these may be outside your geographic region. Nevertheless, creating as many options as possible is sensible in the early stages of your job search.

Remember that you will not receive responses from many of the companies to which you have sent your CV. This may not be a reflection on you, but on them. They may be too busy or they may not have the systems in place to respond. Be patient and resilient. This is probably the most frustrating part of the job search process but with persistence, success will be achieved. However, it is always advisable to contact the company or recruitment agency if you have not heard from them after a period of about two weeks of sending in your application.

Some people will have access to part-time or temporary jobs. This may be in a field outside their normal area of working. Is it worth taking one of these on a full-time basis as an interim solution? This obviously depends on your circumstances. Leaving aside social welfare and income considerations, it may be a beneficial interim solution, provided it does not significantly interfere with your job search. Having somewhere to go everyday and remaining in useful employment helps restore confidence and encourages a sense of well-being. The additional experience may also prove useful. However, it should be regarded as an interim step, not as a permanent solution.

CHAPTER 8

Creating a Winning CV

Any action that aids your search for a new job is valuable and a good CV is crucial to your success. As already stated, spending time preparing your CV is time well spent. Do not be afraid to get assistance with its preparation if you feel it necessary. When an employer is looking for an employee, at least one of the applicants has to be successful. The prospective employer will form their first impression of you from your CV. When evidence of your suitability is presented in a clear, attractive and concise way, this can be a very powerful influence working for you.

What is a CV?

Simply put, a CV is an outline of a person's educational and work history, including achievements and interests. Prospective employers and employment agencies will require a CV. Also, if you are starting a business and are looking for funding, then the funding agency will likely require your career details.

There is no one absolute best way to prepare a CV but there are three guidelines that should be followed:

1. Keep it simple

2. Ensure that what is included is accurate and clear

3. Keep it concise – as short as possible.

Your CV should be:

1. Neatly typed

2. Carefully laid out

3. In black and white

4. Not more than three sheets of A4 quality paper

5. Proceeded by a covering sheet with your name on it.

Where necessary, get your CV typed and photocopied by a secretarial service. In many cases, your former employer will provide this service free.

Some general tips to make your CV stand out:

- Be positive in your language and presentation

- Highlight your achievements with specific short examples

- Make sure that the achievements relate as far as possible to the key requirements, where they are known, of the new job.

Things to avoid when creating a CV:

- Use of jargon or pretentious language

- Telling untruths about your skills or achievements

- Inventing information

- Copying someone else's CV

- Rambling on about a particular aspect.

When preparing a CV with a particular employer in mind, start by finding out what the employer is looking for and tailor your CV to this as far as possible. If you are replying to an advertisement, you will find various clues to the employer's requirements therein. Remember, therefore, to read the advertisement carefully. If you are unsure, try contacting the employer directly for clarification. Better still, talk directly to individuals in the company and ascertain exactly what the requirements of the job are.

Many companies, particularly if they are using recruitment agencies, will send out standard forms, on request, for you to fill in. Having your CV already completed will enable you to answer the questions posed in these standard forms easily and concisely.

What do you put into a CV?

The following headings are normally included but should be varied depending on the circumstances.

Personal details

Put your name, address and telephone number at the beginning of the CV so that your contact details cannot be overlooked. This makes it easy for an interested employer to get in touch with you.

Name

Written as: Patricia Duffy

Middle names are unnecessary, as they will only confuse the reader. Do not use initials, as they are difficult for the reader to remember.

Address

Always use your full address.

Telephone number

Always include your telephone number if you have one. An interested employer may just want to pick up the telephone to talk to you. Do not use a work number unless you have established that it is appropriate to do so. Include the full STD code and number, for example 01 8765432. List your mobile number and your e-mail address if possible.

Date of birth

You are not obliged to give your date of birth. If you wish to, then '15 July 1953' looks clearer than '15.07.53' or '15/7/53'. Use your date of birth rather than putting your age. Employers may be genuinely interested in your age and there will be an opportunity under 'Additional Information' to add more details about yourself.

Nationality

For some jobs, this information is very important. If you are from another country, it is essential that you specify you are able to work here: for example, 'Nigerian (with full Irish work permit)'. Refugee status is also worth mentioning.

Education

In this section, outline your educational history from school onwards. The longer it has been since you achieved a qualification, the less relevant it will be. School and any advanced education information are usually put in chronological order, with your first school coming at the top of the list, finishing with the most recent.

You should include information on:

1. The dates that you attended school – either just the years or the months and years

2. The name and location of the school(s) should be included, although the whole address is not necessary

3. Examinations passed or, if none were taken, the subjects studied

4. Prizes or scholarships attained – this may set you apart from other candidates.

College details should be provided in the same way.

Employment

This section should include information on the different jobs that you have done. You need to research the start and finish dates of all your previous jobs, including part-time, holiday and voluntary jobs, particularly if you have had not much employment experience.

For this section, the order of your employment history is reversed. Begin with the most recent job, list them all and end up with your first employment. This is important because it is likely that your current/most recent job is of most relevance and that it requires more responsibility than your previous positions.

Before you start to describe each job, try to think of all your tasks and responsibilities and make a list. Even though it may seem obvious that a clerical officer would do some typing, it may not be clear to anyone who has not done that job before – and it may be just what the employer is looking for in a CV.

When you have done this, list each job, specifying the main duties. These duties should be presented in note or bullet form, beginning with a verb, for example word processing, typing and so on. If you were in charge of other people in a job, make sure that you mention this at the beginning of your duties and include any promotions that you received during your time in the job.

If you have had many different jobs, remember that the important fact is who you are now and what skills and experience you have acquired. Jobs from further back may show your breadth of experience, in which case they can be grouped together: for example, 'I have four years of payroll and accounts work with agencies throughout the Dublin area.'

It is not recommended that you include details either about why you left each job or the salary you earned. If the employer wishes to find out these things, they can be discussed at interview.

Certain jobs may require particular attributes or competencies: for example, attention to detail may be important for a job in a laboratory; leadership, organisational or team working skills for a supervisory position; analytical skills in a research position; and interpersonal and communications skills in customer service. As far as possible, mention the skills and competencies, whether they were acquired inside or outside of work, which relate to the position being sought.

Interests

Your interests can help to show that you have a well-rounded personality. Any interest that you have or have had in the past that is out of the ordinary will help you stand out. Activities or achievements that make you stand out will help you differentiate yourself from other candidates. Include some physical activities as well as cultural interests. If you belong to any clubs or professional bodies, mention them here. Do not be too specific about any political or religious interests. Overall, you are trying to show the interviewer that you are a well-rounded and balanced person with a range of interests and hobbies.

Additional information

This section can be important if you have gaps in your CV. For instance, you may have taken time-out from paid employment to raise a family or to go travelling.

If you have particular skills outside those already mentioned that are relevant, they can be mentioned here. These might relate to driving, first aid, computer skills, organising or team leadership.

This section also gives an opportunity to explain your particular interest in the job and type of work for which you have applied.

References

You should name at least two people who can be approached to provide a reference for you. Alternatively, you could just state that the names and addresses of referees will be provided at interview; this is generally satisfactory, unless otherwise specified.

One reference should be your last employer and this is why it is so important that you get a good reference when made redundant. Care in selecting the right references is important, as a weak or poor reference will strongly undermine your chances of being successful. Make sure that your referees are happy to be contacted by a number of people, which may be necessary if you are applying for more than one job. Provide the full address and telephone number for the referees. Inform the referees beforehand in the event that they are likely to be contacted. Testimonials are useful but it is likely that your prospective new employer will want to speak directly to your referees. Therefore, it is important that the referee is able to respond quickly to any request. Otherwise, this may delay your appointment or, even worse, put an employer off your appointment altogether.

Preparing your CV for electronic transmission

As stated earlier, more and more CVs are being electronically stored, whether you send it in hard copy or electronically. This poses the question – are there special requirements for CVs as a result? *The answer is yes*. In today's electronic age, you not only need a hard-copy CV that is capable of being easily scanned but also an electronic CV – specifically a text-based e-mail CV. This obviously requires a bit of explanation.

To understand what is needed, let us look at how the process works. When a recruiter in a company wants a CV for a particular job, they will go to their keyboard and type in a job title. Current software packages will provide a list of key words that describe particular aspects of the job, words such as information technology, public relations, design, construction, electrical, welder and so on. Similar to an internet search, these key words are designed to help the recruiter narrow the field of possible candidates so they end up getting as close as possible to correct fit with the job they wish to fill. Including these key words in your CV is therefore vital.

What words should you use?

One way of identifying what key words you should use is to look at the papers and see what words are used frequently in advertisements for jobs allied to that which you are seeking. If you have a job specification, then the key words within will help you.

What format should you use?

If you send your CV electronically, then it will go into the database automatically. However, if you send it in paper form, it will have to be scanned and this relies on the software that the company uses to scan. Sometimes, this software is quite limited. To ensure your CV is capable of being scanned and looks well, the following guidelines should be followed:

- Do not use too much colour or have heavy borders – just use plain white paper

- Avoid using columns

- Use 12 point print

- Italics and underlines should be avoided, if possible.

If you are sending your CV electronically, you will need to convert your CV into a text or ASCII version. This is not difficult to do but, if you are in any doubt, it is advisable to ask someone who is familiar with computers and word processing to do it for you.

How should you distribute your CV?

Having compiled your CV in electronic text version, you can distribute in at least two ways: you can send it to CV banks or to specific people. CV banks are databases or huge numbers of files that store the CVs they receive for later retrieval. Obviously, sending your CV to specific people has the best chance of success, as human eyes will view it before it is put into a bank.

The covering letter

In normal circumstances, a CV will be accompanied by a covering letter. This will state clearly:

- Why you want the particular job in question
- How, in very brief terms, you are ideally suited for the job
- What particular strengths you have that ensure you would excel in that position.

In today's busy world, a covering letter has to get to the point fast. In the past, a hard copy letter might have extended to two or three paragraphs. However, today's electronic world suggests that one screen length is best, otherwise the individual viewing your letter will have to scroll down. This means that your letter should consist of four or five sentences, depending on their length. There are usually three messages you wish to convey:

1. Why you are making contact
   'I was referred to you by ...'
   'I was excited by your advertisement ...'

2. Why your CV should be read
   'My CV perfectly matches your requirements because ...'
   'My success in selling to the same industry as outlined in my CV ...'

3. Suggest what the next step should be
   'I will telephone you to arrange a meeting.'
   'I would be delighted to attend for interview.'

Your covering letter should be put into text version, just like your CV. It is likely that you will need a number of versions tailored to suit the requirements of the employer to which you are sending them.

It is possible that your covering letter will be discarded. Nonetheless, it is worthwhile putting in the effort to ensure the covering letter enhances your chances as a candidate.

The follow-up letter

Another time that it may be appropriate to correspond with the prospective employer is after the interview, particularly if supplying additional information in response to questions raised during the interview would support your case. This will show your enthusiasm. While being careful not to overdo it, your follow-up can be longer than your covering letter, as it is going to someone you have already met. Make sure you end any follow-up with a request for another meeting.

Confidentiality

Confidentiality will be a concern for many people. It is not possible to guarantee absolute confidentiality with CV banks but there are a few useful guidelines to follow to maximise your protection:

- Reputable sites will have a privacy statement, so read it

- Ensure you can remove your CV whenever you want to

- Check on who owns or operates the site

- Make sure the site is password protected

- Do not put information on your CV such as your RSI number, driving licence or passport number.

You can take more extreme measures but these may require specialist expertise and could be an added cost.

Case Example 8

Joan worked for a computer company in the administration department and was made redundant when it closed down. She started applying for jobs and sent out her CV to about twenty companies. She received only two positive responses and went for interview. On each occasion, she was unsuccessful. This made her very depressed.

She decided to seek help and met with a career guidance counsellor in her local FÁS office. The guidance counsellor examined Joan's CV and pointed out that it did not highlight her achievements and was poorly laid out. She discussed with Joan the interviews she had attended and how she had got on. Joan felt that she had been quite nervous and probably did not sell herself well.

Armed with this information, Joan set about revamping her CV and decided to undertake a number of practice interviews. She knew also that she had not made much preparation for the interviews and vowed if she got the chance again, she would do so. She sent her revamped CV to a recruitment agency and to FÁS. She was interviewed by the recruitment agency and after a couple of weeks she was put forward for interview with a large company. She did her homework and rehearsed the interview with friends. She felt confident going to the interview and felt she was well capable of doing the job. She performed much better and was called back for further interviews. Eventually, she was offered the job and she accepted it.

In her new job, there was an emphasis on training and development and she availed of this to move into sales and marketing, progressing her career and developing her self-esteem.

CHAPTER 9

The Selection Process

Preparing for the interview

If you have been working hard at the job search but have not had any success, you may begin to feel frustrated. Regrettably, this is to be expected and it is at this stage that you should bring your natural resilience to the fore. You may also be worried that it has taken much longer than you thought to get a response from the applications you have made. Unfortunately, this is all too common but it may not be a reflection on you. Organisations can take time to receive and sift through what may be hundreds of applications, to line up busy personnel for interview panels and to respond administratively.

Suddenly, one day, a telephone call, letter or e-mail will arrive requesting that you attend for interview. Hopefully, it will be your first choice company. Even if it is not your first choice, it may be worth responding to boost your confidence, as a fallback position and to practise your interview skills. If, however, you have decided that you have absolutely no interest in the job, then this will likely show through at the interview and could do your reputation more harm than good.

Being a good interviewee and showing yourself in the best possible light requires particular skills. These can be learned and, as with all skills, practice makes perfect. For those who either have never gone through an interview process or have not done so for a long time, this can be a daunting prospect.

The job interview process can be confusing. There may be a whole series of interviews with people asking questions that, in your mind, do not make a lot of sense. Like most things in life, you will meet good and bad interviewers. Just because they are on an interview panel does not mean they are skilled. Realising this fact will help to reduce any fears you may have and to take each interview on its merits.

In most cases, interviews will be directly with a company. In other cases, it will be with a recruitment agency. Slightly different approaches are taken in each case.

Interviews with recruitment agencies

The recruitment agency may be interviewing either in general terms as part of a process of registering you on their database or for a specific position with a company. If it is a general interview, the emphasis will be on assessing you and your personality. They want to get a feel for the type of work you like and are capable of doing, and the type of organisation where you would fit in and be successful. When it is for a specific position, treat it as a first interview.

It is important to build a relationship with the agency, convince them that you are worth their effort, that any time they spend putting you forward will be time well spent. Making the best impression with an agency may mean being more flexible, demonstrating that you are keen and proactive. They will then see you as motivated and easier to place.

Remember, when being interviewed by a recruitment agency, you may be dependent on them but they are also dependent on you to earn fees from placing candidates with employers. So, in practice, there is a mutual dependency and benefits. The more jobs they can match to your skills and experience, the more likely they are to get you a job and earn their fee from the employer.

Recruitment agencies can give useful advice. They may be able to advise you on areas that would improve your chances of getting a job and give you valuable feedback on how you performed at the interview. Avail of this advice when the opportunity arises.

Interviews with employers

Interviews direct with the employer will generally be more specific and related directly to the needs of the company. From the employer's perspective, they will be trying to decide whether to progress your application and to establish if there is a good fit with their requirements. From your perspective, you will be assessing whether you really want to work there.

Making the right impression will demand proper planning and preparation. Begin by finding out as much about the company, its products and services as you can. Look up their website – this is one of the easier ways. Get their catalogues or fliers, if they have any. If they have products in the marketplace, become familiar with them. Try to meet someone that has worked or is working for them. Elicit as much information as is feasible about the way they do business, what they value in employees and what the people at all levels in the company are like. If you are going to be working in a particular section, find out how many are in the section, what skills are required and the role that section is perceived to play in the success of the company. If you have not received a job profile, contact the company and ask that one be sent to you. It is also useful to identify:

- What the key roles are in the job

- What the objectives are that need to be achieved

- Whether there are particular requirements concerning safety, hygiene, accuracy, confidentiality and so on.

This information will enable you to orientate your CV and interview answers towards the key requirements of the job and highlight your strong track record in performing roles of a similar nature successfully.

Analyse what information you have collected and identify how your strengths match with the company's requirements and if you have any likely weaknesses. This will enable you to prepare a strategy for the interview in terms of what to emphasise and how to counter questions in relation to your weaknesses. The fact that you went to the trouble to do this will be a practical demonstration of your interest and will impress people accordingly. It will also give your confidence a much-needed boost and ease your anxieties.

The interviewer will have a number of concerns that they will want to clarify.

1. Do you want the job?

2. Have you the basic skills and qualifications?

3. Will you fit in to the organisation or section?

4. How do you compare with other candidates?

5. Will you stay?

Interviewers are only human; they will have biases and prejudices – we all do. This may be unfair but, unfortunately, it is a fact of life. If they like you, they will be more likely to rate you better. Being friendly, courteous and professional will therefore be advantageous. Give each question as much respect as you can.

If possible, get some practice at being interviewed. You only have a relatively short time to make an impression and it is important that you use this time well. No one would go on stage or play an important game without some practice beforehand. Rehearsal with a trusted friend or family member is time well spent. List out the questions you might be asked and practise answering them, particularly those that may concern your weaknesses.

The interview itself

There will likely be two types of questions: closed and open. Closed questions will be specific and you will be directed to give one answer. This will probably be related to your CV and your work experience. It is important that you answer these questions clearly and concisely, so have your facts ready.

Open questions are generally used to encourage you to talk about yourself and your ambitions. Questions such as 'Where do you see yourself in five years' time?' are frequently asked. Be careful not to waffle, undersell yourself or contradict what you have on your CV. The key is to maintain focus and be consistent, bearing in mind the job you are seeking.

Needless to say, arriving on time for the interview, checking if necessary that the time is correct and presenting the best possible physical appearance are important, if not vital. If a secretary or receptionist receives you, make sure you are courteous and friendly. Sometimes, the interviewers ask the receptionist for their impressions. While, it may not be decisive, it may be a factor in final selection when there is little between the candidates.

The first seconds of the interview are of prime importance. Many argue that decisions are often made at this time. A lot of things happen in a very short space of time:

- Entering the room
- Seeing the interviewers for the first time
- Waiting to be introduced
- Maintaining eye contact
- Giving each member of the interview team a firm handshake, if appropriate, and a warm smile

- Sitting down when asked

- Getting yourself seated as comfortably as possible

- Trying not to lean too far forward or back and keeping your hands resting in your lap.

Rehearsing this phase and keeping in mind a positive picture of what it will be like will help you through this period.

Listen carefully to the questions. Checking understanding if necessary and answering clearly will help you make the right impression. Try to maintain eye contact with the interviewers when giving answers. Being nervous is fine but try to turn that nervousness into positive energy. Smiling as you wait helps relaxation. Sometimes, a little self-disclosure about yourself and how you are feeling can be helpful, but do not overdo it or you might appear weak. When people are nervous, they tend to speak faster than normal, so you may need to make a conscious effort to slow down your speech a little.

At the end of the meeting, you will be asked if you have any questions. Have at least two or three prepared. These should be sensible, the last one being about when you are likely to hear the outcome of the interview. Sample questions at the end of the interview are:

- Where does the position fit into the company?

- Is there a performance appraisal system?

- Are there training and development opportunities?

- Are there any planned changes in products or services?

- What is the organisational structure?

Express your deepening interest in the job, how it appeals to you and how you know you can achieve success in it. Shake hands and thank each individual before you leave. Try not to dally too long, but do not rush.

Assessment centres

Assessment centres are a process not a place. They are undertaken usually in addition to the interview and have grown in popularity over recent years, though – in one form or another – they have been around since the Second World War.

Interviews have a notoriously low reliability – between one chance in three and one in four of selecting the right candidate. This may be some consolation if you have been unsuccessful at an interview, as it is possible that the company made the wrong choice. For an employer, however, selecting the 'wrong' candidate is a major source of concern in terms of the resulting cost, lost time and hassle.

In an effort to improve the chances of selecting the right candidate, assessment centres try to simulate the real work situation that you will be faced with in your new job and see how you manage or cope. In other words, they look at the future whereas interviews primarily focus on the past.

So what can you expect if you are asked to participate in an assessment centre? Normally, you will be with a group of other candidates for a series of tests or assessments. These tests are designed to show the employer if you have most of the skills you need to do the job well. Each assessment centre will have a different set of tests depending on the requirements of the job. Examples of some of the tests you could face are:

- Technical skills, such as typing, answering the phone, IT and so on

- Logical thinking

- Decision making

- Analytical ability

- Leadership

- Response under pressure

- Interpersonal skills

- Planning

- Dealing with complaints

- Ability to work as part of a team

- Negotiating

- Selling

- Self-confidence

The exercises that you will be asked to do may be group or individual. Group exercises usually involve being required to discuss a topic or solve a problem. They are designed to see how you perform in a group and focus on interpersonal skills such as assertiveness, leadership, organising or planning. Individual exercises focus more on your personal abilities and skills. Individual exercises can include composing an essay, reviewing and making comments on a case study, repairing a device, dealing with an 'angry customer' on the telephone or solving a problem.

Case studies are often used and sometimes can cause difficulties. A few pointers for handling them are:

- Read it carefully

- Note the key points or messages

- Answer the question you are asked

- Keep to the time limit

- Explain the logic behind your thinking

- Make a decision – it is better than appearing indecisive

- Try to remain calm.

In attempting any task in an assessment centre situation, there are some useful guidelines:

- Make sure you understand the task fully

- Decide on the priorities

- Remain assertive with others

- Compromise where necessary, having made your point clearly

- Be mindful of the time

- Be sure to make contributions but make sure they are constructive and relevant

- Be courteous and retain your self-control.

The fact that you are with other candidates who are competing with you may put a strain on proceedings. It is advisable to ignore this and focus on your own performance. Always be courteous to other candidates and remain positive and professional, even if provoked. Remember that in an assessment centre situation, it is *how* you do things that is important. Since the tests are often designed to show how well you can work with people, seeing it as competition could harm your chances.

Psychometric tests

Psychometric tests can be used on their own or as part of the assessment centre process. They are designed to improve on the chances of selecting the right candidate. Psychometric tests attempt to measure whether you have or have not the specific skills or the appropriate personality traits required to do the job. There are two main types – aptitude and personality tests.

Aptitude tests

These are essentially tests that assess how well you perform against a given standard. They cover such aspects as:

- Ability
- Intelligence
- Performance
- Aptitude
- Problem solving
- Skill
- Verbal or numerical reasoning

They generally require correct answers to specific questions and will be timed and administered under examination-like conditions. It is generally difficult to complete them within the time so make sure you do not get flustered – work at a steady rate without delaying too long on any question.

Like most things in life, practise doing these tests will improve your performance. A little research and practice will be valuable and worthwhile. There are many books published about them and there is a wealth of information on the internet.

Personality tests

Personality tests are designed to assess your personal qualities or traits and whether these will enhance or hinder your ability to perform well in the job for which you are a candidate. These tests identify certain aspects of your personality such as values, motivation and interests. They are designed to explore the way you do things, how and why you behave in certain circumstances, your attitudes and your preferences.

You will be asked to complete questionnaires and the results will then be compared with the outcomes of another group known as the norm group who have taken the tests in the past. There are no right or wrong answers. It is best to be honest, give the answer that feels most right to you and not the one you think your employer might like to hear.

There are a few guidelines worth remembering:

- Remain calm (relaxation exercises are covered in Chapter 11)

- Get as comfortable as possible

- Read the questions carefully

- Follow the instructions

- If you are not sure, clarify

- Work steadily

- Do not spend too long on any question

- Focus on yourself; ignore others

- Keep an eye on the time

- If you cannot answer a question, move on and come back to it later

- Generally, try not to guess – it is about quality not quantity.

Make sure you ask to get feedback on the results whether you get the job or not. They are useful in informing you about yourself and will help in making decisions about your career later on.

Research has shown that the combination of interviews, assessment centres and psychometric testing can increase the chances of selecting the right candidate to a level of seven times out of ten. It is still not perfect but obviously far better than the chances with interviewing only, at just three chances in ten.

Getting an offer

You have now gone through the arduous process of being interviewed and assessed. You will have formed a view of the job and the company. If you have concluded that the job really does not suit you, you may be better to withdraw gracefully from the process, stating in positive terms why you are doing so. Better to do this, if possible, than to end up in a job that leaves you unhappy and dissatisfied for years to come. If you remain excited about the new position and the company has decided to make you an offer, then this is the best possible outcome. The fact that you have an offer will be a great relief to you.

This may be just an opening offer and there may be room to negotiate. Try to establish on what basis the offer is made. Is it related to a particular scale or based on market rates? It may be based on the lowest rate that the company thinks it can get away with or the same figure you had in your previous job. If it is on a clearly established basis such as market rate, there may not be much room for negotiation and attempting to push things too far may be looked on negatively. Doing your homework is helpful – you can check with recruitment agencies, recruitment sites, the newspapers and magazines to see what is the going rate.

Hopefully, you will not have disclosed your desired wage in your CV or during the interview, as you will have disclosed your position and therefore will have less opportunity to negotiate. Do establish in your own mind what you feel the minimum acceptable salary is but, before disclosing your hand, wait for the company to state its position. If the issue is raised, deflect attention by saying how interested you are in the position. Try to make them feel good and that you really want to work for them. While being polite and reasonable, be assertive in asking them to consider some flexibility with regard to the offer. Listen carefully to any response and see what room there is to manoeuvre. If you sense little room remains, establish the shortest time possible for the terms to be reviewed. There may also be additional ways to get your desired package through fringe benefits such as health insurance, pensions and bonus schemes.

If you have any doubts about the offer, then you are better to take time to think it over. They might be disappointed, so provide some reassurance to them.

Finally, if you are happy to accept the position, then do so in a positive manner.

CHAPTER 10

Setting Up Your Own Business

If you have been made redundant, one of your options is to start your own business and become self-employed. You may have a lump sum you can invest in a new venture. There may be opportunities to sub-contract back to your former employer as mentioned earlier. Perhaps you always wanted to become your own boss and you have an idea that you would like to explore.

However, before you start your business, it is worth taking some time to look at your decision from all the angles. Only then can you know you are making the right decision for you and your family. Starting your own business is a life-changing decision, not for just you but for your family also, as they will be directly affected. It is important to know up-front if your personality, life circumstances and finances are consistent with your dream of becoming your own boss and taking control of your life.

Looking at personality traits

Anyone can start a business. In fact, there are nearly two hundred thousand businesses operating in Ireland. Although 97 per cent of them are small, they range from large multinational companies to single-owner businesses with only one employee. Those that are successful tend to have a number of common traits:

- Willingness to work hard

- Belief in themselves and their product or service

- Willingness to learn

- Creative around problem solving

- Resilient

- Persistent

- Attention to detail.

Some of the questions you might ask yourself include:

- Are you good at planning and organising your time?

- Can you handle multiple projects and issues at the one time?

- Have you the physical and emotional strength to deal with the long hours and uncertainty of starting up and running your own business?

- Do you have good negotiating skills to be able to deal with clients and suppliers in particular?

- How comfortable are you dealing with professionals such as bank managers, accountants or people you will meet in the course of your business?

- Are you able to make decisions on your own and follow them through?

- Do you have the passion and resilience to carry on when the inevitable difficult times come?

Other characteristics that are useful but which may be acquired from others are:

- Aptitude to understand and appreciate financial records and accounting procedures

- Ability to understand basic legal requirements in relation to tax, employment, contract, environment, safety and health laws.

If you have only some of these characteristics, it is possible to find ways to compensate through additional training, partnering with someone else or hiring someone. Studies of business start-ups have shown that the most successful ones have more than one promoter with similar values and beliefs and complementary skills. But be careful in selecting partners. If the prospective partner is an acquaintance or a friend, being in business with them will likely change the relationship. People will react differently under the strains of a business situation than in a social setting.

Make sure that your own personality is suitable to running your own business. Consider too that perhaps it would be prudent to resume your career within an existing organisation with an eye to internal promotion. It is best to put both options on the table and weigh up objectively which one suits you and your current circumstances best.

Looking at technical knowledge

In Chapter 4, assessing your capabilities was covered and this will help you decide the types and levels of skills you possess. While it may not always be apparent, every business requires a level of technical knowledge. Whether you are in the retail trade or the technical services area, absence of knowledge will prove a handicap. It is important to assess exactly what key technical knowledge the business will require and to identify where your strengths and weaknesses lie.

Sometimes refresher training will be adequate. Other times, you may need to expand your repertoire of skills. There are many courses available through FÁS and the Institutes of Technology or, alternatively, from plant and equipment suppliers. Getting the necessary training will be important before you launch the business. It is a steep enough learning curve and prior preparation is therefore essential.

Depending on the business area, you may not have to know everything yourself. It may be enough to know someone that has the type of knowledge you need or you may need to include in your plans someone that makes up any deficits.

Looking at practical business skills

Practical business skills are needed to succeed in business, just as driving skills are required to take charge of a car. The owner of a business must have the basic skills to steer it, particularly through the critical early stages. These skills essentially fall into two categories: planning and administration.

The business plan

Before setting up the business, a business plan is essential. If you are seeking assistance from banks or state agencies, they will require you to produce such a plan. However, the most important reason you should create a business plan is that you will be investing considerable finance and time of your own. The business plan allows various possibilities to be looked at without incurring any real cost. Potential dangers can be assessed so that contingency plans can be made to overcome or avoid them. Delays in orders materialising, in jobs starting or collecting monies owed are a normal part of any start-up. Allowances must be made for these and other delays.

When drawing up a business plan, you will need to think through the various elements that are required to make the business a success and what financing will be required. Make sure that your business plan is realistic. It is natural to be optimistic when starting out, and this should be so, but being over-optimistic is foolish and could be self-defeating. A balanced judgement of your prospects will be better for you in the long term.

Getting help with a business plan is a very good idea. County Enterprise Boards and local accountants can be very good sources of advice and assistance. Local chambers of commerce, banks, credit unions, FÁS and Enterprise Ireland are other sources of advice.

Layout of the business plan

A business plan can be a relatively simple document or quite detailed. This will depend on the complexity and size of the business and who you are trying to convince to support you. As a minimum, you will need to state the following in the business plan:

• Nature and description of the business including services or products being offered

• A brief profile of the promoter(s), including track record

• What capability and experience you have

• Who and how many will be employed

• Management structure and organisation

- Objectives (in the form of turnover, number of customers and profitability and so on)
- Targeted customers
- Who and what competitors there are
- How you will achieve the sales
- Why these customers buy from you and not from others
- Profit margins anticipated
- What physical facilities you will need
- A statement of sales, costs and profits or losses
- A statement of cash flows such as receipts from customers, capital investment and payments to suppliers, wages and overheads and loan repayments
- An estimate of the funding and its sources required to support the business in detail over the first year and approximately for the subsequent years.

Presenting the plan in a professional and clear manner will help you make the right impression and increase your chances of obtaining the capital you need to launch your business. It is a sign of your commitment. Make sure it is typed and laid out well. The content should be clear and concise. All assumptions need to be stated so that the projections made can be easily understood and so that it is clear how the various elements such as sales, material, labour and other costs were calculated.

Dealing with the banks

Dealing with the banks can be a tricky business for start-up promoters with plenty of potential pitfalls. Whenever they receive plans from start-up promoters, their rule of thumb is to divide projected sales by two and multiply costs by two. This is based on long experience and is important to bear in mind. They assess both the promoter(s) and the business idea with equal weight and at times give more weight to the promoter(s).

Security on any loans given to business whether in the form of personal guarantees or charges against assets will be as important as your ability to repay them. For limited companies, if possible, try to avoid giving personal guarantees. Realistically, this may be unavoidable in a start-up situation.

Administration

In the rush to establish a business, setting up basic administration systems is often overlooked. These are required for legal and tax reasons and, more importantly, to enable you to see precisely how you are doing and to control the business.

Firstly, there are basic documents such as invoices, purchase orders, pay slips and so on. Then filing systems and an accounting system must be established. Relatively cheap computerised systems are available or, alternatively, you may decide to contract the bookkeeping system to your local accountant or bookkeeping service. Whatever way you approach this area, it is important to gain an understanding of how the system works.

It is advisable that time is allocated each month (at least one day) to deal with administrative matters and to understand/ calculate how the business has performed for that period. Finding out too late that costs are greater than you thought or that receipts are less than you had planned could be disastrous. Dealing with issues upfront and speedily can mean the difference between success and failure.

Funding your business

You may feel you have a great business idea and have the traits and abilities to be successful, but you may not have the funding to do so. The first place to look for funding is to yourself: you may have a lump sum or savings. The second place to look is tax rebates. There is an incentive known as the Seed Capital Scheme. The relief only applies to those setting up in manufacturing, tourism, a trading operation selling goods abroad, certain shipping ventures, some research and development activities and, in certain cases, the cultivation of crops in greenhouses.

An individual who has a sound business idea in any of these areas can make a back-claim for tax relief over the previous five years up to a maximum of about €158,000 as of 2003. The rebate does not exclude the individual from claiming other grants or incentives from the state. A key-qualifying element is that the person setting up the business has been employed with at least three quarters of their income having come from paid employment. Obviously, if the venture is being set up with other individuals, they will also be expected to provide part of the seed capital.

The next port of call for seed capital should be the state agencies. For smaller ventures, enterprise boards may be of assistance. Larger ventures with export potential can look to Enterprise Ireland, Shannon Development or Údarás Na Gaeltachta, depending on the region in which the business will be located. They all have qualifying criteria, so it is best to familiarise yourself with these before making an application. Ask them and they will be happy to advise you. They may assist with grants that enable you to reduce your funding requirements from other sources. For suitable businesses, Enterprise Ireland also may provide loans in the form of preference shares or take direct equity participation.

Business Innovation Centres provide support mechanisms for attracting private finance and will also help you to prepare business plans.

There are a number of Enterprise Centres located around the country. While generally not providing seed capital, they do offer low-cost accommodation/premises and other facilities such as free advice and shared secretarial services.

Certain business opportunities may attract venture capital from other sources such as institutional providers, but this tends to be rare, unless the scale of the proposed business is quite large and the plans very ambitious.

Make sure before you start the business that you have adequate capital. If you do not, it will be even more difficult to raise additional capital if the business has been slower than anticipated to achieve its targets.

Getting emotional supports

So far, the focus has been on what external supports have been available. However, starting a business can be scary. You will be depending directly on your own efforts to generate an income. During this time, you need a support system to keep you on track and to clarify your ideas. In many cases, your family will provide this support. In some cases, this may not materialise because of their own fears. Trying to involve them and being as open as possible will generally enlist their assistance. Friends may also be helpful, but be aware of their limits and possible prejudices. If you decide to attend classes, sharing with other participants can be constructive.

You are on a steep learning curve. Unfortunately, there are

many occasions for you to take the wrong turn or to neglect some critical aspect of the business. Learning from people who have been down this road before is a useful strategy. Getting yourself a mentor is an effective way to ease you through the early stages. This may be from an experienced businessperson from your own network or from panels set up by the County Enterprise Boards and Enterprise Ireland. In any event, it is important that you generate as much support as possible, particularly in the early stages of business.

Exploring your business idea

Having a business idea is a good start but researching the idea properly is vital prior to launching your business. Before you start writing down your business plan, begin by describing your product or service as clearly as possible. The question here is, 'What exactly will you offer the prospective customer?' Some long-established businesses even have difficulty answering this question. You will need to communicate clearly to other people what exactly you are offering so they can recognise that it fulfils their requirements.

As you write your description, you will probably find gaps in your description or in the logic of what you are offering. Spending a little extra time thinking through your idea will help clarify matters and get you focussed on the key issues. For example, if you are considering offering a contract maintenance service, you will need to describe in some detail the nature and scope of the service. Questions you might ask in this instance would be:

- Will you be providing emergency or routine maintenance?

- Will it be on a retainer or hourly charge basis?

- Who will provide the tools and materials?

- Is it plant or building maintenance?

- To what sectors will you offer your service?

- What guarantees of satisfaction are you offering?

As soon as you can articulate your offerings precisely, and with as few words as possible, then you are well on the way and you can build your business plan around what is now a clear and concise concept.

Being all things to all men is not a good idea. Businesses that are successful and profitable focus on a particular niche. Choosing the right niche is critical. Ideally, it should be one from where you can establish a competitive advantage over everyone else. This advantage might be speed of response, a technology benefit or some service element that is difficult for other competitors (now and in the future) to copy.

Talking to potential customers and listening carefully to them will help you to select the right niche. There is a temptation at this stage to defend your idea. However, it is far better to avoid this because you may have omitted a key point or feature from your offering or you may need to enhance it if you are to be successful. Remember you are looking for honest feedback. Find out also what they consider the most important – functionality, price, service, quality delivery and so on.

Learning from your competitors and what they are doing is another good source of information and learning.

- What special features are they offering?

- How are they getting the business?

- What are they doing right?

- On what basis are they doing business – price, quality and service?

- How do they sell?

- What service levels do they give their customers?

- How could their offering be improved?

- Is there something unique you can offer that would make a difference?

The assessment made above will feed directly into your business plan. Decisions can then be made in relation to:

1. What basic resources are needed to get the business off the ground?

2. What form of company should be established – sole trader, partnership or limited structure?

3. What is the likely level of sales?

4. Do you need premises?

5. Can you work from home?

6. How fast can/should the business grow?

7. Is an office and administration manager needed or can you outsource this service?

8. Does the image of the business have to be of a particular type or will it largely depend on you?

9. What is the best way to promote the business?

10. How many people, if any, do you need to employ?

When taking on costs, it is vital that those of a fixed nature are kept to a minimum.

Some, such as insurance and telephone rental, may be unavoidable. The higher the fixed costs, the more vulnerable the business will be to a slower than expected sales growth or to any downturn. This is because it is very difficult to reduce fixed costs even if sales are lower than expected. It is far better to have a relatively small amount of sales and make a profit than to have a large amount of sales and make a loss.

For those providing a service, the quality of clients will be a major determining factor of success. Clients that know exactly what they want, will pay a fair price and, vitally, will pay on time are the bedrock of any service business. These clients will expect and deserve a high level of service. Commitments to them will have to be fully honoured so be careful not to promise something you cannot deliver.

Looking at different business models

When setting up a business, there are a number of business models.

Sole trader or partnership

This is fine for small businesses and professional services. It has relatively low overheads and administration costs. However, you are fully liable for all the debts you incur.

Limited company

This has certain administrative burdens, such as filing returns, but your liability is limited in most circumstances to the money you have invested, provided you act within the law, do not give personal guarantees and comply with the various regulations. Institutions such as Enterprise Ireland require you to form a limited company before they part with investment grants.

Franchise

Getting started from scratch will take time and one way around this is to buy into franchise. This has the advantage that a successful business model, together with the systems of operation and marketing, has already been established. There are now a large number of franchises available. We are all familiar with McDonald's, but everything from carpet cleaning to printing can be franchised. For those looking for an opportunity, unsure what way to go, it is worth looking on the internet or contacting the Franchise Association for further information.

Co-operative

These are set up with producers coming together or workers forming a co-operative. The former is a long-established type of co-operative, with the agricultural co-operatives being prime examples. Workers' co-operatives largely arise out of closures after which a number of former employees come together to carry on at least part of the business. FÁS has a unit to advise on this area. They have met with mixed success. This is because of their inability to raise adequate capital and the fact that they tend to operate in very competitive and declining market sectors.

Networks

A more recent invention, though perhaps they have existed for some time in one form or another, are networks. These involve a group of individuals or indeed organisations coming together to bid for or undertake larger contracts.

Many larger organisations, including government departments, want one tender or want a complete project undertaken by one entity. This saves time on tendering and administrative costs. However, since no one individual can service the full contract, it makes sense for a group to be formed for the specific project. The group is usually disbanded afterwards but can be reformed with a different mix of expertise and resources for other projects.

Many companies now operate on the basis of carrying one or two core functions and sub-contracting the rest. For example, a company might concentrate on product development and marketing and contract out manufacturing and logistics. Even large companies like Benetton do this, but it can apply equally to smaller enterprises. This allows for the promoters of the business to concentrate on what they are good at and leave the non-core areas to others who are geared to deliver them.

So think carefully about which model best suits you and the business.

Case Example 9

Patrick worked in the maintenance department of his company, which was now downsizing as a result of trading difficulties. He had particular knowledge of one large piece of plant and the company was reluctant to let him go. He was concerned that the company might close anyway and he had been talking to the manufacturer and distributor of the machine to see if any vacancies existed within their company. They had indicated that part-time work existed at present and that they could guarantee at least three days' work per week.

While Patrick's company was not offering much in terms of a redundancy package, he was more concerned about having no income if they closed. He had a mortgage and young children. He approached his current employer and made a proposal to him that he would contract back his services at an agreed rate provided they guaranteed him two days' work per week. The company agreed to this arrangement. He set up his own company and contracted his services to the machine supplier and his former employer. He set out to seek work with other companies and employed an assistant on a part-time basis. Luckily, he obtained a number of other contracts, as his former employer went into liquidation less than two years later. By that time, Patrick had built up a strong business base that went from strength to strength. Patrick's foresight saw him through what could have been a very difficult time.

CHAPTER 11

Managing Stress

Understanding stress

As already stated, being made redundant in itself is a very stressful experience. Facing the unknown, deciding on the best course of action, doing interviews, planning a new business venture or further education can add to the stress levels. Even without all these challenges, advances in technology and communications have had a significant impact on organisational life, as well as life in general. The country has more jobs, more people, more variety, higher incomes, new infrastructure and new ways of doing things. At the same time, the pace of life has increased, as have traffic congestion and commute times to work. Expectations in the workplace have also risen and become more demanding.

These stressors can push people into making hasty decisions without considering all their options. The result can be a less than satisfactory outcome. Successfully managing your stress will help you enormously as you move through the transition to a new career. To do this, it is useful to understand what stress is all about and how to develop strategies to reduce and manage it. The challenge of controlling or managing this stress/distress for some can be more difficult than it might first appear.

The concept of stress

Stress can be seen as both positive and negative. It is not always negative and in fact is sometimes necessary for good performance. It is a healthy, natural response and only becomes an issue when the stress crosses the line to distress. Reasonable levels of stress allow us to harness energy and bring it to bear on the task in hand. However, given the differing nature of individuals and how they experience life, getting that balance right is often difficult.

What is stress for one individual can be a good level of motivation for another. The challenge is to achieve a state of mind where it is at an optimal level. If that balance is not achieved, an individual moves into territory that feels uncomfortable, uncontrolled, possibly frightening and overwhelming. What is needed is for individuals to be aware of their responses to stress and recognise them as a choice that can be made. The line beyond which stress becomes negative is not always easy to recognise. As a result, stress can be quite insidious and feel very 'normal'.

When does stress become distress?

Stress becomes distress when the positive pressure that motivates or enhances performance and effectiveness becomes negative, with the result that a person no longer operates at their best. Stress can be defined as an excess of demands over an individual's ability to meet them. A lot has to do with how the person perceives the situation. Since everyone perceives things differently, the response will be different for each individual. A wide range of elements including personality, past experience, internal beliefs, self-esteem and confidence affect perception and interpretation of situations and events. All of these have an impact on how an individual responds to stress and the effects of that response.

Responses to stress

Responses to stress take a number of forms; these can be grouped into three categories: physical, emotional/psychological or behavioural.

Physical – the fear, fight, flight response, the symptoms of which include tense muscles, panic attacks, palpitations and increased heart rate, sweating, colds and illness, aches and pains, upset tummy/nausea, problems with digestion and feeling exhausted. The difficulty arises when the stressful period is perpetuated and the body remains in this state of arousal and tension.

Emotional/Psychological – characterised by anxiety and worry, edginess, loosing temper easily, inability to switch off, feeling gloomy and depressed, blaming, irritability, boredom, feeling unsociable, withdrawing into ourselves, feeling suspicious, inadequate, depressed or angry and exerting pressure on ourselves – 'I must be able to do this', 'I should be able to cope' or 'I ought to try harder'.

Behavioural – the symptoms of which can be difficulty concentrating, replacing creativity with adherence to rules, reduction in output, poor memory, drug taking, absenteeism/ lateness, difficulty making decisions, social withdrawal, procrastination, sexual problems, judgement impaired, making mistakes and being unable to concentrate or decide on priorities.

A person's reaction to the requirement to deliver something small can be completely out of proportion and cause physical and emotional discomfort. Once in that state, it proves difficult to function positively or effectively. One common reaction is avoidance and procrastination – putting things off until the last moment or hoping they will go away.

Try to analyse and define for yourself what exactly the fear is. A common answer is a concern about how you will be seen and evaluated by others. The fundamental fear is that the evaluation will not be positive. This is supported by a strong inner voice saying, 'I cannot do this adequately or to the level that is expected', 'There is an expectation that I have knowledge that perhaps I do not possess' or 'I will let myself down and not show myself in a good light'. Interview situations notoriously generate these sorts of feelings. Thinking about what generates this fear in yourself will be helpful in finding coping strategies that suit you and achieve what is known as healthy state.

What is a healthy state?

For any individual experiencing stress on a consistent basis, a key question must be 'What constitutes a healthy state and how do you go about achieving it?' Words that spring to mind to describe a healthy person include harmony, balance, poise and composure. This is based on the assumption that we each strive to reach our natural capability by whatever means are open to us. The journey for this aspiration gives our lives direction and purpose.

Much has been researched and written about this. Carl

Rogers, an expert and renowned psychologist, carried out a lot of research in this area and he concluded that a 'Fully Functioning Person' or a healthy person has three characteristics:

1. **Increasing openness to new experiences** – a lack of defensiveness. Because the individual does not need to defend against any experience that might occur, they are better able to acknowledge and express feelings and be open to the experience.

2. **Increasing trust in themselves** – due to their better knowledge of their feelings and attitudes, they make and rely on their own decisions. They have developed a sense that doing what feels right proves to be a competent and trustworthy guide to behaviour that is truly satisfying. It includes accurate awareness, unconditional self-regard and generally harmonious relationships with others.

3. **Confidence in your assessments of situations** – individuals look more internally when making choices, decisions or judgements and less to others for approval. The person lives fully in the moment.

Generally, the person is open and comfortable with continuous learning and development. To become healthy, there are two key requirements: self-awareness and self-acceptance. Many psychological tests are designed to increase your self-awareness. One such test is the Occupational Stress Indicator.

Occupational Stress Indicator

The Occupational Stress Indicator is an instrument developed by Cooper, Sloan and Williams as a management tool to investigate and manage occupational stress. The elements that underpin the model of stress upon which the Occupational Stress Indicator is based include sources of stress, individual characteristics, coping strategies and effects of stress, both at an individual and at an organisational level. The Occupational Stress Indicator test can be sourced from a number of providers, many of which advertise in the *Yellow Pages*. Ideally, the company from which you are being made redundant will provide access to them. Make sure they have a licence and are qualified to administer them. There will be a cost.

Of course, psychological tests are by no means the only way to increase your self-awareness. Self-reflection and reviewing your reactions in certain circumstances will be helpful. Getting feedback from respected colleagues and friends is also useful but do not forget that this feedback may be biased by their own prejudices and personalities.

The awareness created by this feedback will enable you to identify strategies for the prevention and management of stress.

Strategies for prevention and management of stress

Stress management strategies generally fall into the following categories:

- Prevention – avoiding stress

- Managing stress – altering responses to stress

- Coping with stress – palliative.

A number of ways of preventing and managing stress are now explored; the first is building yourself up through self-talk (the way you talk to yourself).

Building yourself up through self-talk

We all talk to ourselves. Some of this self-talk will be positive but on too many occasions it is negative. Listening to what we say to ourselves and making this more positive is a powerful way to improve personal effectiveness.

Personal effectiveness is concerned with self-perceptions of how well you can cope with situations as they arise. Unlike the general concept of self-esteem, self-efficacy is situation specific. Coping in some situations causes little or no problems. For example, talking to people in a one-to-one situation may cause you no difficulty. However, making a speech in front of an audience may be terrifying. So the situation is very important in terms of the anxiety it causes.

Self-perceptions of effectiveness influence our thought patterns, performance, motivation and ultimately our anxiety. When the perception that internal standards set by the individual are not met on a regular basis, then distress arises. This causes further anxiety and negative self-talk. A malign circle then ensues which can deteriorate over time to a level where stress turns into distress

There are numerous self-help books and motivational programmes based around this psychological concept. We are all conditioned or programmed from our upbringing. Some of this is good and beneficial; some of it blocks our development. There is a need to delete or replace much of the negative conditioning that is received in the growing-up process when the 'don'ts' and the 'cannots' tend to outweigh the 'dos' and 'cans'.

Self-talk – negative to positive

Negative self-talk is very common and identifying it can be more difficult than might be expected. To change negative self-talk to positive self-talk, a number of shifts must occur.

- Negative talk uses the language of 'I can't', for example 'I could not do that', 'I can never seem to lose weight'. It expresses everything from our simplest misgivings to our greatest fears, fosters self-doubt and chaos, has an effect on our greatest aspirations and can result in an acceptance of just 'getting by'.

- One step removed from this is recognition of the need to change, which can sometimes be associated with words like 'I should' or 'I ought to'. However, there is a tendency to follow these words with 'I won't' or 'I can't', which lead us straight back into negative acceptance.

- To change self-talk, you must examine carefully and change the way you say things that support negativity or thinking negatively. This is the first step, the beginning of positivity and reframing the 'cannots'. The subconscious mind will start to react differently when faced with a challenge – it will begin to think 'this is not a problem'.

- From this platform, you can move to what might be termed the 'new improved you' – characterised by words such as 'I am', where you create the way you want it to be by replacing the 'I cannot' with the 'I am'. One example would be changing the script of 'I can never seem to catch up with things' to 'I am always up to date with work'.

- The final level is one of universal affirmation characterised by language such as 'it is'.

The challenge is to delete the programmes associated with the negative levels and develop the skills relating to the positive. Once this is done, a further challenge is to practise constantly the new skills and language until they become automatic. It has taken a long time for the negative programming to be embedded and it will take time to replace it. Only with practice can this be done.

Practical application – actioning your self-talk

In changing your self-talk, you are setting out to create a long-term vision and belief in relation to yourself and to build a script to support that. Positively and in the present tense is how you should talk to yourself. Therefore, it is important, in developing the script, to use the present tense as you begin to create the new person towards which the subconscious will work.

A further consideration is that self-talk can be internal or external. It is possible not only to sabotage yourself silently but also to do it aloud. In order to change self-talk, you must become aware of it by listening very carefully to how you are talking for a few days. Some statements that you make will be obviously positive or negative talk; others may have passed unnoticed until now, and these are key.

It is necessary to write down a limited number of the significant self-talk statements you make most frequently and to change your language to reflect a positive view, even of negative things. It is surprisingly difficult to do this consistently. For example, rather than saying 'Things are going terrible' you should reframe this and say 'Things could be better', representing the future that you want. Practise these positive statements until they become an automatic response. You will do this consciously at first but, after a while, the positive statements will enter into your subconscious mind and change your perspective. Becoming aware of how difficult this is in relation to external self-talk (the conversations that we have with ourselves aloud) makes it easy to understand how challenging it is to change the internal self-talk.

It is very useful at this stage if you have friends or acquaintances who have a positive outlook on life and whose 'talk' is positive in nature. Seeking them out and being in their company will help you. Modelling individuals whose talk is positive will make the transition easier and encourage you as you progress in your 'reconditioning' process.

Sports psychologists teach sportsmen and women to live in the moment. They do this in the belief that if we can focus without the distraction of thinking about the future or the past, then we will perform much better. This requires practice but has a basis of common sense to it. Stress prevents us from doing this. By reducing our stress, we become more effective. The more effective we are the less stress will impinge upon us. Creating this benign circle will help us through our major life transitions such as redundancy.

Improve focus by limiting concurrent tasks

Today's environment encourages doing everything at speed, doing more than one thing at a time, always moving, impatient, measuring success with quantity and so on. This invariably causes higher levels of stress and many people are actually unaware of their behaviours. Taking time to reflect on how you complete the various tasks that you must accomplish is worthwhile.

A few practical strategies worthy of consideration are:

- Structure the day to address one task at a time and schedule it in the calendar

- Increase likelihood of success by managing the various distractions that would impinge on that by allocating them specific times

- Identify and utilise quiet space when reading, concentrating or planning.

In addition to providing more structure in the day, this is likely to enhance your feeling of control over the situation, which is a key factor in reducing stress.

- Prepare a to-do list that identifies everything that needs to be completed in the day

- Prioritise in terms of importance and secondly in terms of urgency

- Set aside a time when interruptions are not allowed

- Do not feel guilty about the 'to dos' that have not been accomplished in the day – put them on top of the list for tomorrow.

Strategies to address symptoms of stress

Even with stress management and prevention, stress is still an everyday fact and its symptoms are experienced on a regular basis. Consequently, it is important to develop strategies to cope with stress when it does arise and to use these in combination with those already put in place to prevent and manage it. There is a general trend in society for individuals to take more responsibility for personal management of stress symptoms. The popular concepts of exercise, relaxation and so on as a means of reducing stress make sense for most people.

Given that stress is experienced as a process of the mind, dealing with stress must begin with your mental approach to it. Many symptoms can be linked to the fight/flight reaction, which is triggered by thoughts that produce the response to fear, which then triggers off the biochemical reaction. Once started this chain reaction is difficult to arrest and often must just run its course.

Options considered which need to be built into regular routines are:

- Relaxation techniques
- Breathing
- Physical exercise
- Diet and nutrition
- Yoga

Relaxation techniques

Many writers today emphasise the power of relaxation as a therapy. It is a practice that can be learned. When the body is under stress, blood pressure may rise, muscles tense and the heart races. Relaxation therapy addresses these symptoms, resulting in decreased blood pressure, heart rate, oxygen consumption and increased alpha wave activity. This alpha wave activity is a deep state of emotional calm sometimes associated with daydreaming.

There are many different approaches to relaxation. Most involve systematically tensing the muscles in the body and relaxing. Some people suggest focussing on one word or one thing. It is interesting to experience how, given time, the body muscles relax. Relaxation can be practised either during the day or at night, to assist in going to sleep.

Relaxation techniques can be helpful in setting and achieving goals to address personal challenges through the process of visualisation. Visualisation is a way of accessing creative and alternative solutions. The increased level of alpha wave activity in the brain generally achieved in relaxation allows individuals to get beyond the 'thinking logical' left-brain state and to tap into the more creative right-side brain activity.

Physical and mental relaxation not only takes care of stress but triggers right-brain activity, through which we can dynamically solve problems, improve performance and bring changes to our life. When you have achieved a relaxed state, you can select the situation that is giving you anxiety or causing stress. Start by thinking with all your senses, i.e. sensations, smells, images, feelings. Which of these senses causes you to feel stressed? The next stage is to consider how you would like to feel about the situation and experience all the senses associated with that state. The emphasis in this process is to access the power of imagination and bring it to bear on the situation. Imagine yourself coping and being successful; do this a number of times. Find a real situation and, having practiced the above process, carry it through the example of making a public speech. Then proceed to do this in a non-threatening environment, such as with friends or in a classroom environment. Repeat in more challenging environments until the stress and fear dissipate.

Breathing

Stress often impacts on breathing. When under stress, our breathing tends to get shallow and we feel discomfort as we cannot take full deep breathes into our lungs. Some experts assert that if an individual masters their breathing, they have the capacity to find a calm place even in the most stressful work environment. Proper breathing is fundamental to good mental and physical health and has been an integral part of many practices such as yoga for centuries. The action of breathing deeply relaxes the muscles in the chest and stomach and increases the level of oxygen in the blood, which has a tranquillising effect. Poorly oxygenated blood contributes to anxiety states, depression and fatigue and makes it even harder to cope with stressful situations.

Learning proper breathing is a challenge. It is difficult to fill the lungs when you are experiencing stress. However, using breathing to calm yourself during the day and to assist in relaxation can prove helpful. Timed breathing, where inhalations and exhalations are timed to a set pattern (whatever is comfortable), can be particularly useful. One exercise that can make you feel relaxed and alert involves breathing deeply while tapping your chest with your fingers, holding the breath while patting your chest with your hands and exhaling using a purifying breath (exhale all breath forcibly through a small hole between your lips). The result is a feeling of alertness combined with relaxation.

Physical exercise

Regular exercise can improve our sense of well-being. Research generally shows that the physically fit person is able to withstand fatigue for longer periods, is better equipped to tolerate physical stress and generally has a stronger and more efficient heart than an unfit person. Research also shows that there is a relationship between good mental alertness, absence of nervous tension and physical fitness. On this basis, the importance of building regular exercise into our daily routines as an important contributor to coping with stress cannot be overestimated.

Walking is a great form of exercise and contributes to a sense of well-being. In addition, it is flexible and cheap. However, involvement in more vigorous sport such as tennis or swimming, where there is a social and interactive dimension, requires prior commitment and is likely to have greater impact as a mechanism for stress management.

Diet and nutrition

When dealing with stress, we all need more usable energy. A common personal pattern when under stress is to comfort eat. With energy levels down, the tendency is to eat higher levels of processed food and lower levels of fruit and vegetables. When individuals are under stress, their need for all nutrients, especially calcium and B vitamins, increases. Poor diet contributes to a poor reaction to stress. Coffee, which contains caffeine, is actually a stimulant that chemically induces a fight/flight response in your body. If you have difficulty dealing with stress, it will actually make it worse.

By focussing on nutrition and diet, you can increase your available energy. Guidelines recommended by experts include:

- Eat more fresh and raw fruits and vegetables

- Eat more complex carbohydrates, as the body metabolises these foods slowly and they provide more energy (vegetables, fruit, cereals, pasta, rice etc.)

- Use soft margarine rather than butter and cut back on saturated fat

- Use polyunsaturated oils in cooking

- Limit cholesterol intake by eating fewer egg yolks

- Cut back on deli-style meats (high in salt and fat) and increase intake of poultry and fish

- Increase fibre intake

- Eat breakfast

- Cut back on whole milk products to reduce fat intake

- Decrease caffeine intake

- Cut back on alcohol.

Changes such as these can make a big difference in how the body responds to stress. It is likely to result in increased energy, which is needed for coping.

Yoga

Yoga is a system of physical and mental exercise designed to instil a sense of tranquillity and well-being in the individual practicing it. It has been practised in India for thousands of years and may date back even further. It is a technique of self-awareness that integrates mind and body. In many ways, it is a system that combines all the techniques of relaxation described above, breathing and exercise. As a practice, it emphasises balance.

A very short period of implementation of such strategies yields results. Recognition of those results and the reason for success is crucial in order to sustain practice and remain within the virtuous circle. It is important not to be overly ambitious and demanding on yourself. Consistency of implementation is what is key. Personal commitment and time are required; without these, you are likely to slip back to where you were.

Case Example 10

Eamonn worked as supervisor in the customer services department of a large company. It was a very busy office. He was very committed and often worked long hours. He frequently found himself quite tired and stressed at the end of the day. A major restructuring following a merger with another company was announced.

What exactly this meant was left unclear for weeks. Eamonn was concerned but felt his job was safe because of his track record of achievement. However, this turned out not to be the case. He and his colleagues were called together and told that their section was closing down. Eamonn felt that his world had fallen down around him. What would he do next? He had never been unemployed before. He had recently taken out a large mortgage. How would he manage to keep up the payments? He had recently ended a long-term relationship and felt quite depressed about it. So many things seemed to be going wrong. The stress of it all meant he could not think straight.

In the days after the announcement, work seemed more difficult. He felt like staying in bed. His anxieties seem overwhelming, so much so that he could not sleep at night. He knew in his heart and soul that this was not the 'real' Eamonn and that there was something wrong. He decided to visit his local doctor, who gave him advice and a prescription for some sleeping pills. This helped a little but he felt he needed more and when he returned to his doctor, he was referred to a counsellor. The counsellor reviewed his lifestyle and identified what caused his anxieties and suggested ways in which he could deal with them more effectively. Part of this involved changing his lifestyle – exercise and relaxation techniques. How he managed his time and the way he set his priorities was also covered. He suggested that he should sit down, set realistic goals and make a plan for his future.

Gradually, as he began to think about the future and to lay down his options, his anxieties started to diminish. With support from company consultants, he got his CV together and started his job search by sending it to recruitment agencies and direct to companies. Eventually he was successful and found a new position which although challenging was significantly less stressful. Whether this was because of the new environment, reappraisal of his priorities or changes in his lifestyle is unclear. The likelihood is that it was a combination of all three.

CHAPTER 12

Effective Personal Change

The 'sensitive line'

In order to bring about change, we need to be open to feedback from external sources, psychometric tests, self-analysis or individuals we respect. If we are not, then we miss a great deal.

The natural tendency is to resist the acquisition of new knowledge or information in order to protect the concept or perception we have of ourselves. There is always a danger that at least some of the new knowledge might be negative, cause confidence to be eroded or cause some damage to our self-esteem. Whetton and Woods (2000), writers on change, have come up with the notion that everyone has a 'sensitive line'. They define this as follows: 'there is a sensitive line beyond which all of us become defensive and protective when encouraging information about ourselves that is inconsistent with our self-concept and we are under pressure to alter our behaviour'. The risk is that, due to such defensiveness, we can become entrenched and self-awareness may not ensue. Becoming aware of this sensitive line helps us to overcome this defensiveness.

The first powerful lesson for the individual is to understand their capacity to receive/hear the information concerning themselves and what blockages there are to receiving this information. The assumption behind personal growth and development is that it will be better than the current status. This implies that the current status is less than perfect and hence evokes a natural resistance to opening up and challenging that status quo.

The natural tendency to resist the acquisition of new knowledge or information in order to protect our self-concept or self-esteem makes self-examination a challenge. There is always the prospect that at least some of the new knowledge might be negative, cause confidence to be eroded, contradict in some way the current idea of oneself. However, this resistance can cause us to become stuck in a rut and reject the opportunity to change.

As mentioned in the previous chapter, Carl Rogers, the renowned psychologist, identified that the two key necessities for psychological health are self-awareness and self-acceptance. Are there ways of overcoming this resistance and making acceptance of the information easier for the individual?

One way is to use some objective standard, which ensures that the information is predictable and controllable, and results in the individual having the potential to check and validate the information (conflicting or otherwise). This is where psychological tests have an advantage.

Another way of overcoming this resistance and making acceptance easier involves self-disclosure and sharing of information with others. This is where reliable and creditable confidants come into play. Coaching and mentoring by experienced people are useful ways of understanding yourself and becoming more self-aware. We are all aware of how sportsmen use coaches and psychologists to improve motivation, to develop new ways of thinking and to rid themselves of bad old habits accumulated over time. In varying ways, we can adopt the same approach.

Redundancy, while posing many challenges, has the one advantage that it forces you to change. You will be moving on to a new environment with different tasks, people and challenges. You will have to make new responses simply because of these changes. Seeing this enforced situation as an opportunity rather than a threat will enable you see the 'silver lining in the cloud'. Change is difficult for everyone. We all have our comfort zones and would like to stay in them. However, to progress, we need to move out of them and move on. We have talked about this being stressful, and indeed it can be, but this should not prevent us exploring new opportunities and new horizons. Otherwise, we limit our potential and our chances of success.

Effective personal change model

In undertaking successful change management, it is sometimes useful to see it as a process that needs to be undertaken in a logical and progressive way. As the old adage says, 'Rome wasn't built in a day', and this certainly applies to personal change. Research has shown that it takes at least twenty-three days (assuming it is not an addiction) to change a habit. Personal development is a lot about changing habits, many of which we are initially unaware that we have. Thus, the need to raise our personal awareness, as covered earlier.

The following constitute the main elements of an effective personal change programme:

- Preparing for change

- Developing support

- Managing the transition

- Maintaining and building momentum.

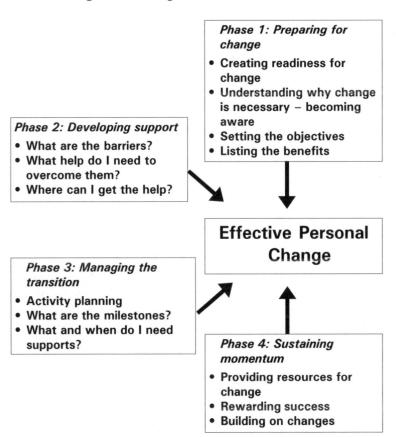

Phase 1: Preparing for the change

Phase 1 is clearly about setting objectives that are realistic but challenging. We need to know exactly what we want to achieve before we set about taking action. A good way of doing this is to think up various scenarios, such as what would various options mean if followed through to the end, what would be needed to achieve the desired outcomes and which scenario would likely be the easiest to implement to get where we want to be. We do this naturally in most circumstances but writing down the various scenarios adds more structure and allows us to revisit them later on and adapt them to suit our needs as we progress.

Getting ready for change is about getting into the right frame of mind and setting about creating the right environment. 'Psyching' yourself up broadly describes what is necessary. Setting down a time point in future when you will start and getting mentally prepared are key to a successful launch of a personal change initiative.

Collecting evidence of why change is necessary to bolster your resolve is important at this early stage. You need as many reasons as possible to move forward. This awareness will come about in many ways, such as internal reflection, exposure to new situations and experiences, feedback from peers and colleagues, and generally by seeking information related to what you want to achieve. By putting a goal in place, you will become automatically more conscious of matters that relate to it. We all have had the experience when we bought a new car; we begin to notice how many models of the same kind are on the road. Our brain, because it has to contend with so much information, automatically blocks out irrelevant information. It only takes on board what we are focussed upon and what is needed to protect ourselves from harm. The minute we set a goal, we facilitate information about that goal to come into our conscious mind.

List out the key benefits of the change and use this list as a support through the period when change is taking place

Phase 2: Developing support

Phase 1 of the exercise is extremely positive and to most people enjoyable. We can use all our creativity and imagination. But we must not be naive. There will be barriers that must be overcome. These might be within us of a psychological and emotional nature. Previous experience and conditioning may be holding us back. It is wise to surface these feelings early and gain as much understanding as possible of their nature and how they will impact on you as you move forward. Being prepared to face up to those 'moments of truth' will decide whether you continue or give up.

Of course, the barriers may be material or physical in nature. Financial concerns, access to supports and other considerations may be a handicap to progress. Being aware of these barriers and building contingency plans will enable you to overcome them or else focus the change programme in a different direction.

If the change is significant in nature, it is unlikely that you will be able to accomplish it on your own without external supports and help. It is better to identify these early on and build them in to your change initiative. This may involve getting counselling, obtaining the support of a friend or family member, or building a new routine. One of the most important supports for bringing about change is to alter the context or environment. For instance, if you want to lose weight, then you will have to alter your dining and snacking patterns as well as the content of what you eat. Remember, if you keep doing the same thing, you will keep getting the same result.

Remaining in the old environment will make change difficult. Altering your environment as much as possible will allow you to put new habits in place and, more importantly, sustain them.

Phase 3: Managing the transition

Managing the transition to achieve your goals requires careful planning that builds in sustainability of effort. There will be times when you falter and your plan should take this into account. Setting out the various actions required and the milestones along the way enables you to break down the change into manageable bites or stages. Each milestone should be seen as an accomplishment in itself and used as a reinforcement to continue on the journey.

Timetabling your actions will give you a clear picture of what will emerge as you progress. Having this clear picture in your mind and a sense of how you will feel at each stage provides a positive motivation along the way. Enlist the supports that you identified in Phase 2. Sometimes, you will find some of your concerns will not materialise as you had thought. At other times, there will be unexpected barriers that you had not foreseen. See these as part of the learning process and face up to them. Build new supports and actions to overcome them.

By continuing towards your goal, you will be surprised at your success. Continually using each success to build your confidence frequently results in the 'snowball' effect. Thus, as you progress, the task becomes easier and the overall likelihood of achieving your goal greater.

Phase 4: Sustaining momentum

It is relatively easy to think up a goal and set about achieving it – it is only when the journey commences that the commitment is tested. This is why so many diets do not succeed – people fail to finish their particular course of action. Sustaining momentum is critical.

What can you do to ensure that this is done? Firstly, by undertaking the three previous phases you will be in a position to take what comes and deal positively with difficulties as they arise. Secondly, by building in a strong reward and reinforcement system, you will create new elements to sustain your progress. These rewards can be visible in nature such as having a night out at an event you particularly like or putting money saved in a transparent container so that you can see it grow. However, rewards should also be emotional, for example in the form of positive feedback from a friend or someone you respect. More often, this feedback should come from your own personal reflection and meditation, and your use of self-talk will be critical to this process. Ensuring your self-talk is constructive and positive is probably the most important way you can ensure that your momentum is sustained. Remember to be patient. Persistence is what will pay dividends. Recognise that it is a journey, and that completing the journey will have worthwhile benefits.

Depending on what level of change is required, the above model can be adjusted to suit your needs. If the change is small, it is still worthwhile planning it, but obviously with less rigour. Where the change is much bigger, such as returning to education or changing career, more careful planning is recommended.

CHAPTER 13

Turning Redundancy into Advantage

Throughout the book, the emphasis has been on treating redundancy as a life experience that can be turned into an advantage. This is easier for some than for others. Realising that you are not alone and that help is there if you know where and how to look for it is important.

Overcoming the initial shock, gathering all your facts and setting goals early on will give you the clarity and confidence to look ahead positively. Taking one step at a time and considering all your options will be far better in the medium term than rushing around without any sense of direction. At the early stage, believing in yourself and your own ability will likely be difficult, so assessing your situation realistically but constructively will give you a sound basis for moving forward.

Remember to seek help and if you conclude that you have a weakness in a particular area, it may be far better to address it at this stage than to ignore it. You now have the opportunity to do this. One of the great problems will be fear of change and of taking on new challenges. While there are no easy ways to get over these fears, they must be confronted, understood and overcome.

Thinking creatively about strategies to do this and enlisting the support of your family and friends will be helpful. Professional help is also available. Many people are shy of seeking such support but the returns can be enormous. Going it alone may be considered brave but, without support, it may be unsuccessful.

You will learn much from each part of the redundancy experience – about yourself and about how you react in certain situations. You will have to develop new coping mechanisms and new ways of dealing with change. This will stand you in good stead as you progress. Remember the lessons from the experience and take time out to consider your career options in the future. Build in opportunities for development and growth. Transferable skills such as those outlined in Chapter 4 are particularly useful as these give greater flexibility for the future. Take advantage of opportunities for training and development. Nurture your career so that you maximise your potential and achieve maximum personal satisfaction from your work life.

At different stages of life, new priorities emerge. Many find it hard to leave behind existing habits and practices and alter their priorities. However, modern work life is forever changing and old guarantees are disappearing. This demands that we adapt and change. It is never too late to change. Outside events, such as redundancy, can be triggers for such change. However, real change comes from within ourselves, not just from external events. Taking control of your life and the changes that you need to make is the best guarantee of realising your goals and becoming fulfilled as a human being.

Appendix

Useful sources of information and support

Legal, social welfare and taxation

⇨ *Notice Obligations*
⇨ *Redundancy Payments and Additional Payments*
⇨ *Selection*
⇨ *Social Welfare Entitlements*
⇨ *Taxation Implications*

- Department of Enterprise, Trade and Employment:
  www.entemp.ie
  → Employment Rights and Industrial Relations
  → Small Business and Local Enterprise
- Department of Social and Family Affairs: www.welfare.ie
- Revenue Commissioners: www.revenue.ie
- Trade Union

Assessing your financial situation

⇨ *Financial Situation*
⇨ *Investment*

- Banks
- Building Societies
- Credit Unions
- Insurance Groups
- Pension Groups

Job opportunities – support services

- Business Innovation Centres
- Community Development Centres
- County Enterprise Boards

- FÁS – Training and Employment Authority: www.fas.ie
  → Community Services
- Irish National Organisation of the Unemployed: www.inou.ie
- Local Area Based Partnership Boards

Training and education opportunities

⇨ *Adult Education Programmes*
⇨ *Sources of Training/Re-Training*
⇨ *Types of Qualifications for Adult Education Programmes*

- Aontas – National Association of Adult Education:
  www.aontas.ie
- Degree Courses – various throughout Universities, RTIs, etc.
- Dublin Adult Learning Centre
- FÁS – Training and Employment Authority: www.fas.ie
  FÁS Training Courses
  → Job Training Schemes
  → Back to Work
  → Start Your Own Business
- FETAC – Further Education Training Awards Council:
  www.fetac.ie
- HETAC – Higher Education Training Awards Council:
  www.hetac.ie
- Master Degree Programmes – as above
- NDEC Oscail – National Distance Education Centre:
  ww.oscail.ie
- VEC – Vocational Educational Committee – local colleges:
  www.vec.ie
- VTOS – Vocational Training Opportunities Scheme

Starting your own business

⇨ *Skills Development – See Training and Education*
⇨ *Support Services*

- Chambers of Commerce – countrywide
- County Enterprise Boards: www.enterprise-ireland.ie
- Enterprise Ireland: www.enterprise-ireland.ie
- Irish Small and Medium Enterprises Association:
  www.isme.ie
- Local Area Partnership – countrywide
- Small Firms Association: www.sfa.ie

Recommended reading

Andreas, Steve and Faulkner, Charles (eds) (1996) *NLP: The New Technology of Achievement*, Nicholas Brealey Publishing.

Arroba, Tanya and Kim, James (1999) *Energising the Workplace: A Strategic Response to Stress*, Gower England.

Benson, Herbert and Mc Kee, Michael G. (1993) "Relaxation and Other Alternative Therapies", *Patient Care*, December 15.

Black, Jack (1994) *Mindstore: The Ultimate Mental Fitness Programme*, Thorsons.

Cooper, Cary L., Sloan, Stephen J. and Williams, Stephen (1990) *Occupational Stress Indicator: Management Guide*, Windsor: NFER-Nelson.

Davis, Martha, Robbins, Elizabeth Eshelman and McKay, Matthew (2000) *The Relaxation and Stress Reduction Workbook*, New Harbinger Publications, 5th edition.

Farnham, Alan (1991) "Who Beats Stress Best – and How", *Fortune*, Oct 7, Vol. 124, No. 8, p. 71(6) Time Inc.

Hall, Calvin S., Gardner, Lindzey and Campbell, John B. (1998) *Theories of Personality*, John Wiley and Sons Inc., 4th edition.

Helmstetter, Shad (1986) *What to Say when you Talk to Yourself*, Thorsons.

Leatz, Christine A. with Stolar, Mark W. (1993) *Career Success/ Personal Stress: How to Stay Healthy in a High-Stress Environment*, McGraw Hill Inc.

Molden, David (2001) *NLP Business Masterclass*, Prentice Hall Financial Times.

Rapple, Colm (2003) *Family Finance 2003*, Squirrel Press.

Rogers, Carl R. (2002) *Client Centred Therapy*, Constable London.

Rogers, Carl R. (1961) *On Becoming a Person*, Houghton Mifflin Boston.

Straw, Alison and Shapiro, M. (2002) *Succeeding at Interviews*, Hodder & Stoughton.

Whetton, D. and Cameron, K. and Woods, M. (2000) *Developing Management Skills for Europe*, Harper Collins, 2nd edition.

Wilson, Paul (1998) *Calm at Work*, Penguin Group.

Yate, Martin and Dourlain, Terra (2001) *Online Job Hunting: Great Answers to Tough Questions*, Kogan Page.

Yate, Martin (2003) *The Ultimate CV Book*, Kogan Page.

Index